FREQUENTLY ASKED QUESTIONS ABOUT CHRISTIAN MEDITATION

Paul Harris
Feb, 2006

FREQUENTLY ASKED QUESTIONS ABOUT CHRISTIAN MEDITATION

THE PATH OF CONTEMPLATIVE PRAYER

PAUL T. HARRIS

INTRODUCTION BY SR. MADELEINE SIMON, RSCJ

© 2001 Novalis, Saint Paul University, Ottawa, Canada
Cover: Allegro168 inc.
Layout: Suzanne Latourelle and Caroline Gagnon

Business Office:
Novalis
49 Front Street East, 2nd Floor
Toronto, Ontario, Canada
M5E 1B3
Phone: 1-800-387-7164 or (416) 363-3303
Fax: 1-800-204-4140 or (416) 363-9409
E-mail: cservice@novalis.ca

National Library of Canada Cataloguing in Publication Data
Harris, Paul T. (Paul Turner), 1926-
    Frequently asked questions about Christian meditation : the
path of contemplative prayer

Includes bibliographical references and index.
ISBN 2-89507-178-0

    1. Meditation–Christianity–Miscellanea.   2. Contemplation–
Miscellanea. I. Title.

BV4813.H372 2001   248.3'4   C2001-902305-7

Printed in Canada.

    We acknowledge the financial support of the Government of
Canada through the Book Publishing Industry Development Program
(BPIDP) for our publishing activities.

10 9 8 7 6 5 4 3 2   10 09 08 07 06 05 04 03 02

CONTENTS

PART TWO

Questions on the Teaching of Christian Meditation 75

PART THREE

Questions About Those Who Have Practised
Contemplative Prayer: Past and Present 107

PART FOUR

Some Questions About the Journey of Christian Meditation/ Contemplative Prayer 179

PREFACE

It is not often one can say, "This is the greatest gift I have received in my lifetime," but that is an accolade I can give unreservedly to the teaching and practice of meditation in the contemplative tradition. I will be forever indebted to the Benedictine monk John Main (1926–1982), whose teaching on the daily practice of silence and stillness in prayer has now grown into the extraordinary contemplative renewal taking place all around the world. Though I never met him, I join many others in recognizing the voice of an authentic teacher of prayer and one of the most important spiritual guides of our time.

Television: no booming voice from heaven

It is now seventeen years since I flicked on my television in early January 1984 and was intrigued by a New Year's Day Eucharist being celebrated at the Benedictine Priory in Montreal. Father Laurence Freeman spoke beautifully in his homily about a daily discipline of prayer that led to an inner stillness beyond words, thoughts and images.

Having worked all my life in the written and electronic communications media, I chuckle at the fact that the gift of meditation was given to me by means of the oft-denounced medium of television and not by a booming voice from heaven. This was a reminder that God usually works through the instruments of other human beings and their inventions. Since that time I have become a firm believer that we should use all the communication means at our disposal to spread the good news of this way of prayer.

After a stint as Director of the Christian Meditation Centre in London, England in 1988–89, I returned to my home in Ottawa, Canada, and since that time have immersed myself in speaking and writing about John Main's teaching; I have also started and I lead two weekly Christian Meditation groups in Ottawa.

The Good News must be communicated

John Main makes the point in several of his talks (200 of which are available on audiocassette) that it is not sufficient to read about or listen to talks on meditation if we do not *experience* meditation itself, if in fact we don't jump into the water and get wet. But the human means of communication we use in handing down the teaching of this way of prayer is of course designed to bring others to the *practice*. The Good News in all its forms must be communicated.

The Question/Answer format of this book

This is why I decided to use a question/answer format for this book; this format has long been a pedagogical way of transmitting spiritual teaching. Jesus constantly answered questions, and in the first letter to the Corinthians, St. Paul answers specific questions from the Greek Christian community that were sent to him in writing.

John Main encouraged questions

It was John Main's custom at the conclusion of his talks on Christian Meditation to encourage his listeners to ask questions about the teaching. While never failing to urge his listeners to "enter into the experience of meditation itself," he nevertheless was aware that for a head-centred generation, a conceptual understanding of meditation was a prerequisite for their "leap of faith" into the practice.

It is in this tradition that this question/answer format is offered not only to those wishing to know more about this prayer tradition but also to those who already meditate. As John Main once said, in meditation we are all beginners and we begin again each day. I hope this book reflects a part of John Main's deep and yet simple teaching on Christian Meditation for newcomers as well as responding to obstacles experienced by those already on the path.

Questions raised over the years

Many of the points and concerns addressed in this book were raised as questions or points of discussion in recent years as I have given retreats, seminars and conferences on Christian Meditation in various countries. It has been my habit to ask listeners to put their questions in writing. From these hundreds of questions I have selected 56 of the most frequently asked questions pertaining to the practice and teaching of meditation. The beauty of answering a question in writing rather than orally is that one can give the time, research and thought necessary for a full response to a questioner. Too often in responding to questions orally, one is forced to shorten answers because of time constraints. There are no trivial or unimportant questions in this book. Some of the questions asked were spontaneous, others well thought out and written down, but I have tried to answer each question in a thorough and thoughtful way.

No one has all the right answers

I should make it quite clear that this book reflects my own personal responses to the basic issues and questions people have raised. Other individuals who give talks on the teaching and practice of meditation might respond in quite different ways. We all see "through a glass darkly" and no one has the absolute right answer to every question. All we can do is speak from our own experience and background in responding to questions.

This way of prayer is not taught but caught

Finally, I offer a reminder that ultimately we can't analyze, dissect or even logically explain the "unexplainable," the often dark path of silence and stillness in contemplative prayer. There is a saying that this way of prayer is not *taught* but *caught.* All I can hope is that each individual reader will, through this book, enter more deeply into the actual daily experience of this way of prayer and be led to that "country beyond words and beyond names."

Paul Harris

INTRODUCTION

John Main says in one of his talks:

The wonderful beauty of prayer is that the opening of our heart is as natural as the opening of a flower. To let a flower open and bloom it is only necessary to let it *be*; so if we simply *are*, if we become and remain still and silent, our heart cannot but be open, the spirit cannot but pour through into our whole being. It is for this we have been created.[1]

This is one of my favourite quotations as it seems to sum up in a few words the innate aptitude for contemplation in each one of us. In meditation we open ourselves to this central silence in the core of our very soul.

Meister Eckhart (1260–1327) also puts this so well:

The Central Silence is there where no creature may enter, nor any idea, and there the soul neither thinks nor acts nor entertains any idea either of itself or of anything else.[2]

This is the simplicity at the heart of the teaching of silent prayer from two great teachers. But even at their most sublime, words always come up short. The Chinese philosopher Hua Hu Ching writes, "The highest truth cannot be put into words." Nevertheless, we must still strive, despite the poverty of our human words, to express the inexpressible, and to pass on this teaching to future generations – always bearing in mind, of course, that the true teacher, Jesus, is always there, invisible in our midst.

This is the gift that Paul Harris has brought more than 15 years as he has tirelessly worked to convey the basic teaching of Christian meditation to audiences around the world. In his most recent book, *The Heart of Silence: Contemplative Prayer by Those Who Practise It* (Novalis,

1999), he gave us the experiences of 60 men and women from various countries speaking openly and freely about their own personal pilgrimage of meditation and how it has affected their lives. This year he reverts to an ancient pedagogical device of questions and answers to convey the teaching in a traditional but easy to understand form.

A fascinating aspect of this book is that questions on individuals range from John Cassian and the early fourth-century desert monks to the American Cistercian monk Thomas Merton; from the medieval anchoress Julian of Norwich to Etty Hillesum, who died at Auschwitz in 1943; from the author of *The Cloud of Unknowing* to Simone Weil, who wrote *Waiting on God*; from the Anglican spiritual writer Evelyn Underhill to the best-selling Italian author Carlo Carretto; from the English Benedictine Bede Griffiths to Jean Vanier, Mother Teresa and John Main.

A quick glance at the lives and teaching of these individuals shows that no religious tradition, no particular age, no particular culture or gender has a monopoly on the spiritual wisdom of silence in prayer. In these men and women we come to realize that the inner spiritual experience of contemplative prayer is the same in all ages: a longing for the Spirit deep at the centre of one's heart.

Caught up in the immediate, the temporal and the passing of our computerized world, we often forget the eternal truths and the spiritual vision of gifted teachers of contemplative prayer, such as John Main. This book will do much to bring a fresh perspective to John Main's teaching on meditation, as well as inform us about fellow travellers in their work of the Spirit.

Madeleine Simon

Sr. Madeleine Simon is a religious of the Sacred Heart in London, England. She founded the first Christian Meditation Centre in London in 1986 and a second centre in Royston near Cambridge in 1988. She first met John Main in 1963; they remained lifelong friends. She is author of Born Contemplative, *a book on how to introduce children to Christian meditation, and has played a pivotal role in introducing John Main's teaching, principally in the United Kingdom.*

PART ONE

QUESTIONS ON THE PRACTICE OF CHRISTIAN MEDITATION

QUESTION 1

Q. How does one go about praying in this way? Is it difficult to master this technique?

A. Well, first of all, meditation is not really a technique. My dictionary defines the word "technique" as a "proficiency in a practical or mechanical skill." But meditation is more than a mere mechanical skill. It is a daily spiritual practice and discipline that opens us up to the indwelling Spirit of the Lord and that bears fruit in our everyday life and relationships.

The "how to" of Christian Meditation, as taught by John Main, is as follows:

> Sit down. Sit still and upright. Close your eyes lightly. Sit relaxed but alert. Silently, interiorly begin to say a single word. We recommend the prayer-phrase "maranatha." Recite it as four syllables of equal length. Ma-ra-na-tha. Listen to it as you say it, gently but continuously. Do not think or imagine anything – spiritual or otherwise. If thoughts and images come, these are distractions at the time of meditation, so keep returning to simply saying the word. Meditate each morning and evening for between twenty and thirty minutes.[3]

The simplicity of meditation

The thing that surprises most newcomers to Christian Meditation is its simplicity. John Main always emphasized how simple it is to enter into the experience of meditation.

As we begin to meditate it is good to become aware of our breathing. Let your breathing slow down and become regular and, as John Main says, interiorly begin to say a single word. He recommends the ancient Christian prayer "Maranatha." "Maranatha" is Aramaic, the language that Jesus spoke, and means "Come, Lord Jesus." Recite it as he suggests, in four equally stressed syllables: ma-ra-na-tha. Listen to it as you say it, gently but continuously.

St. Paul ends the first letter to the Corinthians with this prayer word, and St. John ends the book of Revelation with it. It is one of the oldest Christian prayers. Biblical commentators tell us it was a password that allowed the early Christians into homes for the celebration of the Eucharist.

Meditation is not what you think

In meditation we do not think or imagine anything, spiritual or otherwise. If thoughts and images come, even holy thoughts, these are distractions at the time of meditation, so we return to simply saying our word. "Meditation," as one T-shirt reads, "is not what you think." *The Cloud of Unknowing* says, "He may be reached and held close by means of love, but never by means of thought."[4]

John Main recommends meditating each morning and evening for between 20 and 30 minutes (20 minutes for beginners), preferably before and after the day's work. It is better, if possible, to meditate before a meal.

In meditation we do not reflect on the meaning of our word as we recite it. The author of the fourteenth-century book *The Cloud of Unknowing* is emphatic on this point:

> If your mind begins to intellectualize over the meaning and connotations of this little word, remind yourself that its value lies in its simplicity. Do this and I assure you these thoughts will vanish....
>
> It is quite sufficient to focus your attention on a simple word...and without the intervention of analytical thought allow yourself to experience directly the reality it signifies. Do not use clever logic to examine or explain this word to yourself nor allow yourself to ponder its ramifications.... I do not believe reasoning ever helps in the contemplative work.[5]

In meditation we come from the head to the heart

If we worry about what we are feeling during meditation, we are courting discouragement. There is no such thing as a bad meditation or a good meditation. Be indifferent to what happens in the actual times of meditation. God does not judge us on how well we say the mantra but on our generosity, our faith, and our surrender to God's indwelling presence. In meditation we want to come from the *head* to the *heart.*

We should not evaluate our progress in meditation, but be assured that meditation will gradually transform our lives into love if we persevere. Above all, we should not evaluate our progress in what happens during the actual times of meditation. Sometimes we will be silent, sometimes we might be totally distracted. If you want to evaluate progress, look to the inner transformation in love that is taking place in your daily life. (See Question 15 on measuring our progress in meditation.)

Listen to the sound of the mantra

As we recite our word we simply listen to the sound. We want to go beyond thoughts. Listening to it as a sound helps our concentration. We try to keep the body as still as possible. We are body, mind and spirit, and stillness of body will help to silence the mind. Of course, there is a paradox here, for stillness of mind will also help keep the body still.

Meditation is simplicity itself. We hold ourselves alert and attentive during the entire time of prayer. As a fourth-century desert father put it, "We centre ourselves, and focus on the God whom we do not see, whom we do not hear, but whose active presence we totally accept." This is where faith enters into our prayer.

It is hard to believe that meditation is really as simple as it seems. We are tempted to complicate it. But meditation does get simple as one goes along the path. Eventually, as the mantra becomes rooted, it will take less and less effort to say it as we enter into deeper and deeper realms of silence.

We watch one hour with Jesus

Meditation teaches us that *being* is more important than *doing*. The *heart* is more important than the *mind*. Our role is to be content with a loving, peaceful openness to God, without concern, without the desire to taste, or cling to, or possess God. We simply listen, watch and wait, even though nothing seems to happen. In the Garden of Gethsemani, Jesus says to his disciples, "Could you not watch one hour with me?" In our daily periods we do watch this one hour with Jesus. In meditation we simply surrender ourselves and rest in God. (See also Question 19 on the Gethsemani sleep.)

Meditation is a daily spiritual discipline

Meditation challenges us to overcome our self-centredness. Can we meditate without concern for where God is leading us? Can we meditate faithfully when distractions bombard us? Can we meditate when nothing "happens" in meditation? Can we give up our desire to possess God and shed all desire for spiritual consolation in meditation?

The practice of daily meditation is also a spiritual discipline. In talking about contemplative prayer, the *Catechism of the Catholic Church* states:

> The choice of the *time and duration of the prayer* arises from a determined will, revealing the secrets of the heart. One does not undertake contemplative prayer only when one has the time; one makes time for the Lord, with the firm determination not to give up, no matter what trials and dryness one may encounter.... The heart is the place of this quest and encounter in poverty and in faith. (#2710)

Say your mantra

In meditation, faith, fidelity, commitment, perseverance and patience are the most important ingredients. We must be gentle with ourselves. We must try to let go and abandon ourselves before the God whom we do not see but whose presence we totally accept. We stand before the Lord and wait. As Father John Main never tired of saying: "Meditation can be summed up in three words, *say your mantra.*"

In the Gospel, the Lord speaks about a mustard seed as a symbol of divine love. It is the smallest of all seeds but grows into the tallest tree with its enormous capacity for growth. In meditation, the repetition of the mantra, this small seed of divine love, has the power to grow within us and to transform us.

Finally, meditation is a way of pure faith. Nothing else. We simply have to put this faith into practice each day.

QUESTION 2

Q. Will you explain in more detail the role of the mantra in this way of prayer?

A. A mantra is simply a sacred word or a phrase that is repeated continuously at our times of meditation to bring us to an interior silence in the presence of the Lord. The aim of the mantra is to bring us to our own centre, our own heart, where we learn to be awake, alive and open to the indwelling Spirit. In this stillness and peace we not only become aware of God's presence, but we *experience* it.

The mantra says to God: I am open to Your presence

In the book *Moment of Christ*, John Main comments on the integrating power of the mantra:

> The faithful repetition of the word integrates our whole being. It does so because it brings us to the silence, the concentration, the necessary level of

consciousness that enables us to open our mind and heart to the work of the love of God in the depth of our being.[6]

The mantra is a spiritual discipline, a help towards concentration, enabling us to go beyond words and thoughts, even holy thoughts. We say the mantra slowly, steadily, with attentiveness. When we find our mind has wandered, we come back to our mantra. There is therefore nothing secret or magical about the mantra. It is simply a daily calling upon God, a spiritual discipline of *love*.

John Main tells us that if we persevere on the path of meditation, gradually the mantra begins to take root. It begins, as it were, to sound in the heart, and we begin to hear the mantra at a much deeper level of our being. The mantra, he says, should be said unhurriedly and calmly, but we must be humble and patient. The mantra says to God, "I am open to Your presence, I am resting in Your presence, I am in Your hands. Do whatever You will with me." The mantra is our surrender to God.

The history of the mantra

The use of a mantra in prayer is found in many of the major religions of the world: Hinduism, Buddhism, Islam, Judaism and Christianity. In the Christian tradition it is rooted in the teaching and practice of the fourth-century desert fathers and continues to this day.

The word "mantra" comes from the Sanskrit words *man* ("the mind") and *tri* ("to cross"). The mantra, practised as a spiritual discipline, enables us to cross the sea of the mind. The sea is another apt image for the mind. Ever changing, the sea is calm one day and turbulent the next. Our minds are drifting about on the surface, blown by every wind on the treacherous waters. We can never make the crossing without some help. That is the role of the mantra.

To use another image, the mantra eventually takes us down to the bottom of the sea, where everything is calm and tranquil. On the surface there may be crashing waves (our mind, our distractions), but at the bottom of the sea it is always quiet and our hearts are calm and silent.

The Christian tradition of the mantra

The Christian tradition of the mantra sprang out of the deserts of Egypt in the fourth century. A desert monk, John Cassian, played a very important role in bringing this ancient prayer tradition of the mantra to the Western church. In his Tenth Conference on prayer, he talks clearly about the repetition of a prayer phrase to bring one to an interior silence. He points out that this was the common practice of the early desert monks. Cassian refers to the repetition of a prayer phrase as a "formula." Today we would call it a "mantra." (See Question 33 on John Cassian.)

The mantra and *The Cloud of Unknowing*

The Christian use of a mantra has continued through the ages since the fourth century. In the 14th century, the author of the famous English spiritual classic *The Cloud of Unknowing*[7] said this about the mantra in contemplative prayer:

> Take a short word, preferably of one syllable. The shorter the word the better. A word like God or love, choose which you like, or perhaps some other, so long as it is of one syllable. And fix the word first to your heart so that it is always there come what may. This short word pierces heaven. This word is to be your shield and your spear. Whether in peace or in war with this word beat upon the cloud.[8]

(See Question 34 on *The Cloud of Unknowing*.)

There are many Christian mantras. The Benedictine monk Henri le Saux, who wrote under the name Abhishiktananda, advocated the word "Abba" (Father) as a mantra, pointing out that Scripture shows that Jesus made it his constant prayer. "Abba" is a word in Aramaic, the language that Jesus spoke. (See Question 37 on Abhishiktananda.)

The word "maranatha" as a mantra

John Main suggests the word "maranatha" as a mantra. (One of the oldest Christian prayers, it is also in Aramaic and means "Come, Lord Jesus.") When St. Paul wrote his first letter to the Corinthians, in Greek, he was able to insert the Aramaic word *maranatha* at the end of the letter. According to scripture scholars, all the early Christians fully understood this word. It was a password that allowed Christians into homes for the celebration of the Eucharist.

Maranatha also appears in one of the oldest existing written fragments of the Eucharist. In the invitation to receive communion, the priest says:

Praise to the Son of David. If anyone is holy, let them come. If anyone is not holy, let them repent. Maranatha. Come, Lord Jesus.

The mantra as a spiritual tool

While "maranatha" is a sacred word to Christians, we do not dwell on the meaning of the word during meditation. We want to go beyond thoughts and images and rest in silence in the Lord. The mantra, therefore, is a spiritual tool, a help towards concentration, enabling us to go beyond words or thoughts, even holy thoughts. It is also a daily discipline. We say the mantra slowly, steadily, with attentiveness. When we find our mind has wandered, we simply come back to our mantra.

Four equally stressed syllables: ma-ra-na-tha

In reciting maranatha we break the word into four equal-ly stressed syllables: ma-ra-na-tha. And we listen to the word as a sound as we say it gently, continuously, for the full period of our meditation. John Main says there may come the day when we enter the cloud of unknowing, in which there is silence, absolute silence, and we can no longer hear the mantra. This absolute silence may last for only a short period of time and then we must return to saying the mantra.

But John Main reminds us that we cannot attempt to force the pace of meditation. We must let go of goals and trying to achieve anything. The mantra will become root-ed in our consciousness through the simple fidelity of returning to it each morning and each evening.

The mantra brings us into the present moment

The great secret of saying our mantra is that it automati-cally brings us into the present moment. When we say our mantra we cannot be thinking of the past or the future. We are inserted in the *now*. If we read the letters of St. Paul we realize Paul was always living in the present moment. He says, "*now* is the hour of salvation, *now* is the acceptable time, *now* is the time to rise from sleep." Not yesterday, not tomorrow, but *now*. The continuous recitation of the mantra brings us into the present moment.

Listen to the mantra as a sound

The mantra should be repeated silently with as much attention as we are capable of giving. The mantra will then descend to the deepest level of consciousness until it becomes as natural as breathing. Again, we listen to the mantra as a sound. Listening to it as a sound helps our concentration to move from *thought* to *being*.

It is hard to believe that meditation and saying our mantra is really as simple as it seems. We are tempted to complicate it. But meditation does get simpler as we persevere on the path. In the beginning we say the mantra at the surface level of our mind, but eventually, as the mantra becomes rooted, it will take less and less effort to recite it. Our work is simply to say it with faith, love and openness to God's presence. This constant daily practice will root the mantra deep in our consciousness. It will become our friend and companion.

Finally, we should always remember that the way of the mantra is not a technique or a method for accomplishing a goal – not even the goal of silence. Silence only points the finger towards God. The discipline of meditation requires faith, trust, letting go, openness, attention, joy and, most important of all, love. Everything else we leave in the hands of the Lord.

QUESTION 3

Q. Can one say the mantra outside of the daily meditation periods?

A. Yes, the mantra can definitely be repeated outside of our daily times of meditation. This tradition ties in directly to St. Paul's admonition to "pray unceasingly" (1 Thessalonians 5:17).

This means that we can take every opportunity during our waking hours, no matter how brief the time, to repeat the mantra. This practice will root the mantra more deeply within us, and it will more quickly become a companion and a friend on our spiritual journey.

Opportunities for saying the mantra during the day

There are many daily opportunities in everyone's life to say the mantra: on the bus going to work, cleaning the house, washing the car or dishes, exercising, brushing our teeth, sitting on a park bench, and many other mechanical or recreational tasks in our daily routine.

However, there are other times when we need to give our full attention and concentration to the task at hand.

There are times when we should *not* say our mantra: driving a car, operating machinery or using dangerous tools, and especially when we need to give our full attention to writing, reading, listening to music, conversation with others, and other concentrated tasks.

Saying the mantra in pain and anxiety

Many people find the recitation of their mantra an aid to falling asleep. The mantra can also be a great source of consolation and strength in times of crisis, trauma and even pain. Meditators constantly talk about the power of the mantra to divert our attention and therefore offer relief from pain and anxiety. But beyond this, when we say our mantra we are calling upon God at the deepest level of our being. This is where our faith and grace enter into meditation.

One meditator recently recounted an incident after surgery. As he woke up after the anaesthesia wore off, he was welcomed by the mantra sounding loud and clear within, without a need to consciously say it. More importantly, he felt it was like an old friend welcoming him back to the land of the living and offering him support and encouragement for the approaching convalescent period.

The mantra in a time of crisis

In a recent article in the *Blue Mountain Meditation Center Newsletter*, Dr. John Hedberg, a physician from Colorado, recalls a crisis in his life that was greatly aided by the recitation of a mantra. Late one Friday afternoon, he received a letter threatening him with a malpractice suit.

"It shakes you to the core," he recalled. "As a doctor your professional integrity is being questioned." He decided to see it as a challenge and a test of his spiritual discipline flowing from the practice of meditation. "I had a chance," he said. "I could let this ruin my weekend with my family or I could seek strength from the mantra."

Throughout the weekend, whenever anxious thoughts began to speed up, the mantra was something he could grab onto to keep his mind still and stay focused on having a wonderful time with his family. When he returned to his office on Monday to start a new week, he says the mantra was a source of strength in responding to the letter in a loving manner. The lawsuit was never pursued.[9]

The mantra is like a brook that murmurs in the heart

Once the mantra is rooted through our daily practice over a period of years, we might begin to hear it sounding within, without having to do all the work ourselves. In the beginning, we repeat the mantra at the surface level of the mind. But as we persevere, the mantra becomes more deeply rooted in our consciousness. We "pray unceasingly." Bishop Theophane the Recluse (1815–94) writes that after the initial effort of saying our prayer word, the prayer becomes like a brook that murmurs in the heart.

The mantra releases a deep inner spiritual strength. When at times the mantra spontaneously arises in our consciousness in our daily routine, this is a great blessing and gift of God. Father John once said, "First say the mantra at the time of meditation, and then [soon] it will begin to sound within at other times of the day."

QUESTION 4

Q. How can the practice of meditation benefit our bodies and our health?

A. An article in *New Scientist Magazine*[10] has estimated that more than a thousand research papers have been published on the health benefits of meditation. Scientists have done innumerable clinical studies on meditators that indicate a lower oxygen consumption during meditation, decrease in serum lactate levels (relaxation), reductions in systolic and diastolic blood pressure, lower heartbeat, relaxation of muscle tension, enhancement of the immune system, and reduction in anxiety levels.

Since we are one entity – body, mind and spirit – we can accept with thanks these physical side effects of meditating. However, what is important to keep in mind here is that any physiological benefits of meditation are quite secondary; one might say they are signs rather than the essential meaning of meditation.

Can meditation battle tooth decay?

Some of the findings on the health benefits of meditation can bring a smile and even challenge our credulity. If your teeth are not up to par, you might take heart from a recent headline in a North American newspaper: "Meditating 40 minutes a day can help battle tooth decay." The article went on to say that studies have shown that meditators have saliva that is lower in acid and bacteria and hence is less likely to decay tooth enamel.[11]

Or how about this? *USA Today* newspaper recently quoted Dr. Herbert Benson, author of several books on meditation, as saying "Thirty-four % of his infertile patients get pregnant within six months, 78% of insomniacs become regular sleepers and doctor's visits for pain are reduced 36%, all through regular periods of meditation."

John Main and physiological benefits of meditation

In his 200 taped Christian Meditation talks, John Main rarely mentions any of these physiological benefits of meditation. Father John obviously felt that lower blood pressure or reduced oxygen consumption paled into insignificance when one believes meditation is a spiritual path into the presence of the indwelling Christ. In other words, Father John felt we must keep our priorities straight. Meditation is primarily a faith-filled spiritual discipline; any positive side effects to the body should be considered as secondary.

However, meditators are often aware of greater physical vitality and energy, which has led to the aphorism that

"Meditators have 25-hour days." In other words, the one hour we devote to meditation is not lost time, for we seem to get the investment of time back with interest even in the physiological sphere.[12]

QUESTION 5

Q. I'm a newcomer. Can you give me some practical tips on how to prepare for meditation?

A. As you know, Christian Meditation is a daily spiritual discipline, a path of faith in which we open our hearts in silence and stillness to the indwelling presence of Christ.

However, from a human standpoint it helps to know a little about the process of meditation. Meditation is essentially a process of stilling the mind and slowing down the rush of thoughts until the mind comes to rest. We often call meditation "resting in God." For the vast majority of us, this process is long, demanding and frustrating.

The mind is like a forest of trees

The mind does not like to meditate; it wants to wander. When we first begin to meditate and try to concentrate, the mind is hyperactive. An Indian sage, Sri Ramakrishna, once said, "The mind is like a forest of trees with monkeys chattering away and jumping from branch to branch."

The repetition of a sacred word or mantra is the primary means of slowing down the mind. But saying the mantra is a discipline. Here are a few tips to help the process along:

- Try to meditate at the same time each day. If you have regular times for meditation each morning and evening, even the mind knows these are times to quiet down. Come to meditation even if you have not slept well. Meditation will help make up for that restless night.

- It is important in the beginning to get into the habit of keeping the spinal column erect in meditation. Head, neck and spine should be naturally in a straight line. This doesn't mean making your body tense, but on the other hand, try not to let your body slump. Keep your hands relaxed and resting on your knees or in your lap. Aside from this, try not to give too much attention to your body.

What to do before meditation

- What to do at the beginning of meditation is a personal choice. Some people ask God's blessing, or say a short prayer out loud in an effort to focus their attention and remind them of the purpose of their meditation. Some meditators read a passage from Scripture. Others simply repeat the mantra a few times. Some people spend a few minutes relaxing and getting into a comfortable sitting position. Others take a few deep breaths. Some people splash cold water on their faces in an effort to be wide awake and attentive. Some people take off their shoes (see Question 9 on taking off one's shoes while meditating). Choose what suits you best.

- Never allow anything to get in the way of your meditation period. Meditation cannot be done in fits and starts. A simple decision will have to be made: "I'm going to put meditation first." Be faithful to the daily discipline of meditation.

- Set aside a room or place in your home to be used only for meditation and spiritual reading. After a while your mind will associate the room with meditation, so that simply entering it will have a calming effect on you (see Questions 6 and 7 on the time and location for meditation).

The virtue of timing tapes

• A question you will have to face is how to time your period of meditation. Many meditators pre-record their own timing tapes, beginning with a few minutes of music, then 25 minutes of silence and ending with music. If you have time slots and dubbing ability on your tape recorder, you can pre-record these tapes with your own choice of music. These timing tapes are available for sale in many countries as well. Timing tapes offer an advantage over electronic timers, whose excessive noise can often send one into orbit. One thing you do not want to do is to keep looking at your watch, which can be a major distraction.

• The best time to meditate is before a meal. The digestive process slows down our ability to be attentive and to concentrate and, of course, in meditation we want to be totally alert.

QUESTION 6

Q. How do I find a quiet location where I can meditate?

A. This can be quite a challenge and often requires the co-operation of spouses or other family members. To ensure quiet, meditators often unplug the phone during their meditation period. Some also put a "Do not disturb" sign on the door of the room.

With regard to location, it is recommended to meditate in the same location each day, if possible. The goal here is to meditate in a place set aside for stillness, a place where you can simply *be.* Some people use a basement or a bedroom; one meditator I know has cleared a small room and equipped it with a prayer bench and a small table with a candle and a Bible. Some people like to meditate outdoors in gardens, parks, and other locations where they feel close to nature. However, the sounds and scents of nature could be a distraction to certain individuals.

On finding a quiet location

The Cistercian monk Thomas Merton writes about the importance of finding a room or some corner for prayer where one is undisturbed and free from the tension that binds one "by sight, sound or thought."

Certainly our surroundings can assist us in coming to stillness. And often our prayer room will be a sign to other family members that we are not to be disturbed in our time of meditation. We have to give priority not only to those daily times but also to our spiritual environment.

The *Catechism of the Catholic Church* mentions that "for personal prayer there can be a 'prayer corner' with the sacred scripture and icons, in order to be there, in secret, before our Father. In a Christian family, this kind of little oratory fosters prayer in common." (#2691)

Sacred spaces

Author Mary Anthony Wagner also points out the importance of a "sacred space" where family members can respect the need for one's silence and solitude. In her book *The Sacred World of the Christian* she writes:

> There might also be a hermitage within the home, a space in which stillness can be assured, a space to reflect, to study, or simply to be alone. This holy space could be a den, a bedroom, or a specific room in the basement which through common agreement would not be disturbed when occupied by its "hermit." Setting aside such space would itself bespeak the significance of taking time to be quiet and alone with God, and of respecting this kind of need and value for solitude in one another.[13]

QUESTION 7

Q. What are the best times to meditate each day?

A. Morning and evening are the traditional times of prayer in most of the world's religions, including Christianity. The monastic tradition in Christianity starts the day with Matins (morning prayer) and ends the day with Compline (night prayer).

Morning meditation

In the morning, nature is usually calm and quiet and brings freshness and renewal. Most people feel the best time to meditate is immediately after getting up, before eating breakfast and starting the day's activities. John Main felt it was always better to meditate before a meal rather than after. In the morning we place God first in our priorities. Before the outer world calls, there is a call to enter the inner world of stillness.

Evening meditation

The evening period of meditation usually presents a greater challenge for most people. Many of us have been involved in the hustle and bustle of the day. Because we all lead such different lives, it is difficult to lay down any general guidelines for the evening time of meditation. Again, if possible, it is desirable to meditate before you eat your evening meal and the digestive process begins. However, this is not always possible and many people choose a later hour in the evening. Some people are night people and are wide awake and can concentrate in the late evening. For others, a late evening meditation would simply result in sleepiness and nodding off.

Sometimes choosing a time for meditation requires ingenuity. A mother of nine children who meditates finds a magic half-hour in mid-afternoon when some of her children are sleeping and other children have not yet arrived home from school.

If you are tired after the busyness and activities of the day, it might be a good idea to take a quick shower or at least splash water on your face before the evening meditation. Regularity and punctuality are important aspects of morning and evening meditation. For this reason it is a good idea to try and build a regular rhythm and pattern of set times to meditate each day.[14]

QUESTION 8

Q. I'm a newcomer to the practice of Christian Meditation. Distractions are driving me crazy. What am I doing wrong?

A. If it's any consolation to you, this is the number one question asked by meditators all around the world. Let's seek the wisdom of spiritual teachers over the centuries about this question of distractions. This is a famous story about two early fourth-century desert monks:

> A brother came to Abbot Pastor and said: Many distracting thoughts come into my mind, and I am in danger because of them. Then the elder thrust him out in the open air and said: open up the garments about your chest and catch the wind in them. But he replied: This I cannot do. So the elder said to him: if you cannot catch the wind, neither can you prevent distracting thoughts from coming into your head. Your job is to say no to them.[15]

The poverty of distractions

In his book *The Contemplative Life*, the Dominican priest Father Thomas Philippe writes:

> When we have the impression that we have spent our time in prayer driving away distractions; when we have been left with our poverty with nothing but this striving for God, we can be sure that God has been acting in the depths of our soul. We perceive it afterward when we resume our other activ-

ities, by a sense of peace and rejuvenation in the depths of our hearts.[16]

Thoughts jostling in your head

Theophane the Recluse, the 19th-century monk, bishop and spiritual director, said this about distractions:

> Thoughts continue to jostle in your head like mosquitoes.... An aid to this is a short prayer, which helps the mind to become simple and united.... Together with this short prayer, you must keep your...attention turned towards God. But if you limit your prayer to words only, you are as "sounding brass."[17]

Distractions and the wandering mind

St. Teresa of Avila (1515–1582) once said:

> Distractions, the wandering mind, are part of the human condition and can no more be avoided than eating or sleeping.[18]

Thomas Merton (1915–1968) reflects on the challenge of distractions in his book *Seeds of Contemplation*:

> Prayer and love are learned in the hour when prayer has become impossible and your heart has turned to stone. *If you have never had distractions you don't know how to pray.* For the secret of prayer is a hunger for God and for the vision of God, a hunger that lies far deeper than the level of language. The [person] whose memory and imagination are...with a crowd of useless or even evil thoughts and images may sometimes be forced to pray far better in the depths of their...heart.[19]

Distractions will always be with us

That's the first great lesson about distractions. They accompany us on our lifetime practice of contemplative prayer. The problem all of us have in coming to an inner silence in meditation is that our minds are full of thoughts, images, sensations, emotions, insights, hopes, regrets – a never-ending array of distractions.

St. Teresa of Avila once said the human mind is like a boat where mutinous sailors have tied up the captain. The sailors all take a turn at steering the boat, and of course the boat goes around in circles and eventually crashes on the rocks. That is our mind, says Teresa, full of thoughts taking us off in every direction. An Indian sage, Sri Ramakrishna, once said that the human mind is like a forest of trees with monkeys jumping from branch to branch, chattering away.

Distractions and the trunk of an elephant

Another pertinent story illustrates the capricious human mind. In India, the mind is often compared to the trunk of an elephant – restless, inquisitive and always straying. In India, if you watch an elephant in a parade you will see how apt the comparison is. In Indian towns and villages, elephants are often taken in religious processions through the streets to the temple. The streets are crooked and narrow, lined on either side with fruit stalls and vegetable stalls. Along comes the elephant with his restless trunk, and in one quick motion it grabs a whole bunch of bananas.

The late Eknath Easwaran, a teacher of meditation, telling the story of the elephant, says:

> You can almost see him asking, 'What else do you expect me to do? Here is my trunk and there are the bananas.' He just doesn't know what else to do with his trunk. He doesn't pause to peel the bananas, either, or to observe all the other niceties that masters of etiquette say should be observed in eating a banana. He takes the whole bunch, opens his wide mouth, and tosses the bananas in stalk and all. Then from the next stall he picks up a coconut and tosses it in after the bananas. There is

a loud crack and the elephant moves on to the next stall. No threat can make this restless trunk settle down.

But the wiser trainer, if he knows his elephant well, will simply give that trunk a short bamboo stick to hold on to before the procession starts. Then the elephant will walk along proudly with his head up high, holding the bamboo stick in front of him like a drum major with a baton. He is not interested in bananas or coconuts any more, his trunk has something to hold on to.[20]

The human mind, says Easwaran, is very much like an elephant's trunk. Most of the time it has nothing to hold on to. But it can be kept from straying into the world of thoughts, imagination and fantasy by simply giving it something to hold on to – a mantra.

How to handle distractions

The mantra is a help towards concentration, enabling us to go beyond distractions, including words and thoughts, even holy thoughts. We say the mantra slowly, steadily, with attentiveness. When we find our mind has wandered, we simply come back to our mantra. We cannot force this way of prayer through sheer willpower. Don't try too hard. Let go, relax. There is no need to fight or struggle with distractions. Simply return to the repetition of the mantra. The key word here is *gentleness.*

But a word of caution. The repetition of a mantra does not bring instant peace, harmony, absence of distractions, or silence. We must accept where we are on the pilgrimage of meditation. We should not get upset at continual distractions. Our aim is not to be free of *all* thoughts. Again, this would be a goal, and we do not want to have goals. John Main constantly advises us not to come to meditation with any expectations. So do not struggle and fret over distractions. The mantra simply expresses our openness to God and his indwelling presence.

We can't force the elimination of distractions

John Main also reminds us that we cannot attempt to force distractions to go away. In fact, we must let go of goals and trying to achieve anything. The mantra will become rooted in our consciousness through the simple fidelity of returning to our mantra each morning and each evening. Meditation is centering ourselves on our inner core and allowing God to pray within us. Says Father John:

> I want now to address a particular question that we all encounter. It is the question of distractions. What should you do when you begin to meditate and distracting thoughts come into your mind? The advice that the tradition has to give us is to ignore the distractions and to say your word and to keep on saying your word. Don't waste any energy in trying to furrow your brow and say, 'I will not think of what I'm going to have for dinner,' or 'who I'm going to see today,' or 'where I'm going tomorrow,' or whatever the distraction may be. Don't try to use any energy to dispel the distraction. Simply ignore it and the way to ignore it is to say your word.[21]

Attention: the other side of distractions

The French author Simone Weil, who died in 1943 at the age of 33, was an apostle of the spiritual life and defined prayer as *attention*. The mantra leads us to this attention. (See Question 39 on Simone Weil.) Another French spiritual writer, the 17th-century French Christian apologist Blaise Pascal, felt the greatest enemy of prayer was the "Gethsemani sleep," when the apostles slept instead of watching with Jesus. Pascal felt that inattention and drowsiness were the enemies of prayer. Again the mantra helps us with this problem by bringing us to attention.

Don't get angry at distractions. This is a non-violent way of prayer. Ignore distractions by continually returning to the mantra. If we are distracted with thoughts 50 times in a period of meditation, when we return to the mantra that is 50 times we have chosen God over the distractions.

A problem often observed by those meditating is that the thinking process continues even while they say the mantra. There is a term for this: *double tracking*. Again, this is nothing to be concerned about. With perseverance, the mantra will become stronger and our thoughts will diminish as the pilgrimage of meditation continues.

It is important to remember that when we are bombarded with thoughts and images at our time of meditation, our will is still tuned in to the presence of God. To handle distractions we need gentleness and patience. We have to wait, like the wise virgins in the Gospel, in patience and hope. Gentleness and patience indicate that the Spirit is working silently within us. While we are aware of distractions, we should never let them disturb us. We can even see the good in distractions; they keep us awake and on the journey. They come in one door and leave by another.

Despite distractions the Spirit is working silently

Stephen J. Rossetti put it well in his book *I Am Awake: Discovering Prayer*:

> We cannot force grace. It is a gift. We can only wait in patience and hope, like the wise virgins. Paradoxically, it is in the waiting that God is often present. Usually, in the very depths of our being, the Spirit is working silently. Our patience and gentleness are themselves signs of this Spirit's presence.[22]

Despite all our efforts, thoughts will come: good thoughts, bad thoughts, "urgent" reminders. Ignore them all. We just keep saying our word silently. We try to let go of thinking. We try to keep saying your word. We repeat the mantra silently and continuously in our hearts. The mantra will lead us to discipline, to concentration, to silence, to God.

QUESTION 9

Q. Is there a tradition of taking off one's shoes before meditating?

A. Many meditators treat the location of their daily meditation practice as a holy place where they enter into the presence of God. Rituals can be important at the beginning of meditation: these might include washing your hands or face, setting a timer for the length of time you wish to meditate, reciting a short prayer from Scripture, or taking off your shoes.

In a holy place it seems to make sense to take off one's shoes, which may carry in contamination, dust and dirt from the streets. On a practical level, taking off your shoes can simply be more comfortable. However, meditators are free to make their own choice in this matter.

The Old Testament tradition

There is an ancient tradition of taking off one's shoes during meditation. In the Old Testament, Moses meets God in the burning bush. The first thing God says is, "Take off your sandals in the presence of the LORD" (Exodus 3:5). Some meditators like to follow this pattern of taking off their shoes "in the presence of the LORD" during their meditation periods. However, it is always optional. For some people this tradition might be a distraction.

We stand on holy ground

In her book *Seasons of Your Heart: Prayer and Reflections*, Macrina Wiederskehr has this beautiful insight about shoes and prayer:

Taking off your shoes is a sacred ritual. It is a hallowed moment of remembering the goodness of space and time. It is a way of celebrating the *holy ground* on which you stand. If you want to be a child of wonder cherish the truth that time and space are holy. Whether you take off your shoes symbolically or literally matters little. What is important is that you are alive to the *holy ground* on which you stand and to the *holy ground* that you are.[23]

QUESTION 10

Q. What role does correct posture play in the practice of meditation? What is the best way to sit?

A. As the psalmist says, even the body longs for prayer: "My heart and my flesh cry out for the living God" (Psalm 84). Because we are a single entity – body, mind and spirit – the body is a companion in meditation with the mind and spirit. For that reason we must respect, take care of and love the body and recognize this union and integration of body and spirit. St. Paul was well aware of this and in the first letter to Corinthians says, "The body is for the Lord, and the Lord for the body" (1 Corinthians 6:13).

In regard to sitting, perhaps Richard Rolle, the 14th-century English hermit and contemplative, has put it most succinctly for Christians:

> Sitting I am most at rest
> and my heart moves upward
> I have loved to sit, for
> thus I have loved God more
> and I remained
> longer within the comfort
> of love than if I were
> walking or standing or kneeling.[24]

Sitting expresses receptiveness, self-surrender and particularly "resting in God." Sitting is an ideal posture for prayer because it roots us in attentiveness while at the same time allowing us to be relaxed. St. Teresa of Avila once said, "We need no wings to go in search of God, but have only to find a place where we can sit alone and look upon God present within us." That is a good definition of Christian Meditation, and note the importance she gives to sitting.

"I am not sitting, I am on a journey"

Here are a few other quotes that emphasize the importance of sitting during prayer.

Philosopher Blaise Pascal once said, "All the troubles of life come upon us because we refuse to sit quietly for a while each day in our rooms." A Zen Buddhist meditation saying reads, "Sitting...sitting and the grass grows greener." There is also the story of St. Sarapion, the Sidonite, a desert father of fourth-century Egypt. He travelled once on a pilgrimage to Rome. Here he was told of a celebrated recluse, a woman who lived always in one small room, never going out. Skeptical about her way of life, for he himself was a great wanderer, Sarapion called on her and asked: "Why are you sitting here?" She replied: "I am not sitting. I am on a journey."

The history of sitting in prayer

For those who associate prayer with their early childhood training of saying their prayers on their knees, sitting in meditation may at first seem strange. Yet this is an ancient practice in most of the world's religions. For 5000 years, Hindus have been meditating in the lotus (sitting) position. Zen Buddhists in particular are noted for sitting in meditation. In Christianity, the early fourth-century desert monks sat weaving baskets or sewing while reciting a biblical mantra.

How to sit properly

In meditation we aim at a harmony of body and spirit. This is where the correct posture of an upright back plays an important role. Correct posture can help us to remain alert and focused in our daily periods of meditation. If the body is steady, alert and still, it strengthens and supports the spirit. We should sit comfortably with a straight back but not stiff or tense.

It is the universal teaching in meditation that a still body is an aid to stilling the mind. This is a primary reason why it is important right at the beginning to getting into the habit of keeping the spinal column (head, neck and spine) erect in meditation. Sitting properly in a comfortable position in meditation allows us to breathe freely in saying our mantra and helps us to be physically still. However, we don't have to keep our body tense in sitting. This straining would only be a distraction. We must balance our sitting with being relaxed. Stillness helps us to realize our bodies are sacred, "temples of the Holy Spirit" (1 Corinthians 6:19). As the psalmist says, "He leads me to still water; He restores my soul" (Psalm 23:2).

On choosing a chair

When you sit in your meditation chair your feet should be flat on the floor. (If the chair is too high, place a cushion or book under your feet.) A straight-backed chair will be the best choice, but its comfort often depends on height or slope. A chair with arms will help keep you from slumping. Look for a chair where you can sit alert but at the same time at ease. If possible, it is best not to let your spine collapse against the back of the chair. Prayer stools or prayer benches are quite popular today because one's legs and back are positioned comfortably in another symbolically prayerful position.

Sitting on a cushion

Some people prefer to sit on the floor on the forward edge of a firm cushion. Your head should remain in line with your trunk (make sure the cushion is not too high or you will pitch forward.) Legs should be folded, not held out straight. Pain and numbness can be a distraction here until you acquire flexibility in this position. Keep your chin tucked gently in, not thrust forward. Keep your shoulders relaxed, not slumped. Rest your hands on your knees or lap. If you have not practised sitting on a cushion, it will be hard to maintain a good sitting position for 20 to 30 minutes. Patience will be required to strengthen spinal muscles and keep hips flexible.

Whether you sit in a chair or on a cushion or prayer stool, the one rule of thumb is to keep your head, neck and spinal column in a straight line and your eyes closed.

Offer your body as a living sacrifice

We do not want our bodies to be in discomfort or pain in meditation. This in itself will be a distraction and will interfere with your concentration in saying the mantra. Having said this, it is obvious that one can still meditate when one is sick or even in pain. Whether it is healthy or sick, at ease or in pain, the role of the body is in the service of the Lord. Speaking to the Romans, St. Paul said, "I beseech you therefore, by the mercies of God to offer your bodies as a living sacrifice, holy, acceptable to God which is your spiritual worship" (Romans 12:1).

Correct breathing is also an important aspect of meditation. It is a good idea to take some deep breaths before meditating and to become aware for a few moments of your breathing. Most people synchronize the saying of the mantra with their inhaling and exhaling. (See Question 12 on breathing.)

No one can doubt the importance of body consciousness in prayer. Witness Christian monks chanting the

Divine Office, Indians praying on the banks of the Ganges at dawn, Moslems prostrate before God at their daily times of prayer, Jews at the Western Wall in Jerusalem or Zen Buddhist monks sitting. St. Paul saw the importance of this when he said to the Corinthians, "Glorify God in your body" (1 Corinthians 6:20).

QUESTION 11

Q. Do I try to make my mind blank or void in Christian Meditation? Is the aim to have no thoughts at all? Can emptying the mind be dangerous? Will it make me vulnerable to undesirable forces or influences?

A. One of the problems we face in the teaching of Christian Meditation is that in speaking about emptying our minds of concepts and images, we might inadvertently give the impression that all that remains is a vacuum or, as you refer to it, a void. Some of the early Christian teachers of contemplative prayer are not overly helpful in this regard. Evagrius of Pontus says, "Prayer means the shedding of thoughts," but doesn't answer the question "What happens next?" [25]

Interior silence: filled with the presence of God

Perhaps it is better to speak in positive rather than negative terms about setting aside thoughts in meditation. The interior silence we open ourselves to in meditation is filled with the *presence* of God. Sometimes it is not a *felt* presence, but the special knowledge we call faith means we can "know" in our times of meditation that the indwelling Trinity actively lives and prays within us. It has nothing to do with making our mind a void or our inner being becoming a vacuum. In meditation we open our entire body, mind and spirit to the direct experience of the Spirit deep within us.

At the still point we find God, who is love

The repetition of our mantra will keep us alert, concentrated and free from any kind of void or blankness. Meditation is based on faith, and this faith will keep us aware of God's presence.

John Main says:

...the fruitful repetition of the word integrates our whole being. It does so because it brings us to the silence, the concentration, the necessary level of consciousness that enables us to open our mind and heart to the love of God in the depth of our being.[26]

The mantra says to God, "I am open to your presence, I am resting in your presence, I am in your hands. Do whatever you will with me." The mantra is our surrender to God. There is no vacuum or void in this way of prayer.

At our "still point" or our "centre," we find not emptiness but God, who is love. St. John of the Cross says, "God is the centre of my soul" and Julian of Norwich says, "God is the still point at my centre." The path to this centre is the way of the mantra and leaving behind our ego, our self-centredness and our self-consciousness. (See Question 29 on the ego.)

The Cloud of Unknowing points out that Satan cannot enter this inner chamber of our heart in this silent prayer. The author says that in this silence one can only be open to the voice of the Spirit who dwells deep within us. (See Question 34 on *The Cloud of Unknowing*.)

QUESTION 12

Q. Is there any special advice on breathing for our daily meditation periods?

A. John Main, with his Irish wit, once said, "The only important thing about breathing is to continue to do so for the full time of your meditation." In John Main's 200 talks on audiocassettes he rarely mentions any particular role of breathing.

In this respect he joins many other teachers of meditation who feel that anything that takes attention away from the recitation of the mantra is itself a distraction. The late Eknath Easwaren, renowned teacher of meditation in California, felt it was counter-productive to give any special attention to connecting the repetition of the mantra with one's breathing or heartbeat. Like some other teachers, he felt that each person comes naturally to integrating their breathing with the mantra and that we should put no special effort into this process.

The body and meditation

Bearing in mind the point these teachers are making, perhaps it is valid to recognize that the body does play an important role in our meditation practice. (See Question 4 on the body in meditation.)

The problem for so many people who come to meditate is that they breathe poorly, so that their lungs are never fully used; only a small proportion of the 70 million alveoli in their lungs are extended. There is a tendency for some people who meditate to breathe shallowly through the mouth and make little use of the diaphragm (abdomen) when they inhale. This results in only the top part of the lungs being used and only a small amount of oxygen being inhaled. Tension usually results from rapid, shallow breathing from the top of our lungs. Our aim in meditation is to breathe slowly and deeply from our abdomen. St. Paul would understand the process in the light of his advice to the Romans: "Make every part of your body into a weapon fighting on the side of God" (Romans 6:13).[27]

No conscious effort required

Breathing in meditation should be a slow, natural rhythmic action involving the entire torso. Ideally, breathing correctly means breathing through the nose with the mouth closed and the lungs fully inhaling and exhaling. Breathing out should normally take twice as long as the in-breath. The more stale air we can exhale, the more fresh air we can inhale. The breath itself should be calm and deep. Deep breathing will calm the nervous system.

As already mentioned, integrating the saying of the mantra with the inhaling/exhaling process seems to come naturally and spontaneously to almost everyone who meditates. Often no *conscious* effort is required. Perhaps this is why John Main was hesitant to emphasize any particular breathing practice. He recognized that without any conscious effort, most meditators adapt the mantra spontaneously to their breathing.

There is no right way to breathe

For those newcomers who wish to have some idea of how to adapt the mantra to their breathing, here are a few examples of how this can be done with the mantra "ma-ra-na-tha." Bear in mind that different individuals will choose different ways, depending on their lung capacity. There is no *right* way to do it. One could, for instance, say the entire mantra breathing in, while breathing out in silence. Or one could say the mantra by breathing in "ma-ra" and breathing out "na-tha." Some people say the mantra only on their out-breath. There are also five or six other combinations, again, usually depending on one's lung capacity.

What is most important is to come to a comfortable rhythmic pattern reciting the mantra in conjunction with your breathing and to build this discipline into your meditative practice. Again, for many people no *conscious* effort will be required to accomplish this. The advice is to let it all happen naturally.

QUESTION 13

Q. Should I feel guilty if I miss one of my daily meditation periods?

A. The only thing to feel guilty about is feeling guilty! There is enough religious guilt among Christians without adding to the burden of guilt.

Fidelity to the morning and evening meditation is important, but there will be times when, through the circumstances of our life or our own lack of discipline, we miss a period of meditation. It takes time to establish discipline, and discipline is a way of liberty, not restriction. Meditators often point out that they feel a gap in their day when this happens. But whether it is deliberate or not, don't feel guilty. Simply come back the next day with renewed commitment to the path. What is important is to hang in there for the long run. A false sense of guilt has no part to play on the path of Christian Meditation. Jesus calls us to repentance, not guilt.

There is, however, an Indian saying about this: "If you skip one day's meditation, it takes seven days to catch up." So make every effort to build the daily discipline into your daily life.[28]

QUESTION 14

Q. Does God speak to us in meditation? Do we hear God's voice?

A. Thomas Merton once said that God's language is silence. So God does not speak to us with a booming voice from heaven but, like Elijah, we will hear God speak to us in the silence.

On the path of meditation we will certainly come to know how God has "spoken" to us. We will see the decisions made, the pitfalls avoided, the right path followed, and we will know that God has spoken to us. But we will not hear the voice of God in our times of meditation in the usual sense of that term. In our meditation periods, God speaks directly to our hearts. God's language indeed is silence.

Of course, when it comes to hearing God speak to us on the spiritual journey, there may be times when we will not be absolutely certain we have heard his voice or what is the right thing to do in certain instances. For this reason we need faith, deep listening, and sometimes the wise counsel of others.[29]

QUESTION 15

Q. How do we measure our spiritual progress in meditation?

A. Evelyn Underhill (1876–1941), who devoted her lifetime to the study of prayer and spirituality, was adamantly against checking one's spiritual pulse. She once said, "It is quite impossible for any of us to measure ourselves and estimate our progress." (See Question 40 on Evelyn Underhill.)

Meditation is all about *not* looking for progress or results. As John Main says, it is about taking the searchlight off ourselves, it is about losing our self-consciousness. If we start asking questions such as "How far have I come?" or "How long is all of this going to take me?" or "Am I becoming holier?" then we are becoming self-conscious – something we want to avoid. Meditation, he says, requires simplicity. We are led to that simplicity by faithfully saying the mantra.

We don't turn to meditation to find answers, to achieve some kind of fulfillment, or to solve the problems of our life. We meditate to become rooted in God, to *be*, to be present to God's inner presence, and in that presence to be transformed into love. Meditation is a spiritual death to our ego and a spiritual resurrection of our inner self to live again in Christ. John Main puts it so well:

What all of us have to understand is that we are not meditating in order to make something happen. We are not meditating in order to get some sort of insight. In fact, we are not meditating to gain any possession whatsoever. Quite the reverse. We are meditating so that we can dispossess ourselves, not just of our ideas and insights but to dispossess ourselves of our very selves.[30]

On measuring spiritual progress

It is also a truism that we cannot measure the spiritual. We can measure the depths of the oceans and the number of galaxies but we simply cannot measure the spiritual in any normal way. The only real test of spiritual growth is an increase in simplicity, compassion and love.

In addition, what happens in our daily times of meditation is not of great importance. Usually nothing happens. Meditation is not about entering into an altered state of consciousness or seeing and experiencing anything out of the ordinary. Wondering about our spiritual progress is really part of the self-centredness we are meant to leave behind in meditation.

Thomas Merton reminds us of this same point:

Do not be overanxious about your progress in prayer. You have left the beaten track and are travelling by paths that cannot be charted or measured. Let God take care of your prayer and your progress in it. Seek only to purify your love of God more and more. Seek only to abandon yourself more and more perfectly to His will.[31]

The only way to evaluate our progress in prayer is to look to the inner transformation into love and compassion for others that is taking place in our daily lives. In this way we can get some sense of our spiritual growth. In fact, it does not take a long time on the path of meditation before St. Paul's fruits of prayer begin their work within us. St.

Paul's "harvest of the Spirit" includes love, joy, peace, patience, kindness, goodness, fidelity, gentleness and self-control (Galatians 5:22). All of these gifts are released to us as we learn to listen to the language of the heart, which is silence. But these gifts extend outwards to others in our family, the community, our work situation and to all aspects of our daily life and relationships. (See Question 49 on the relationship between prayer and action.)

Returning to the marketplace

The only questions we can ask about progress are these: Are we being changed into the fire of love through meditation? Is there an integration of action and contemplation? In Zen Buddhism there is a series of pictures that depicts our spiritual journey as a search for an ox (a symbol of enlightenment). In the last picture, the seeker finds the ox and immediately returns to the marketplace of everyday life, an integrated, enlightened human being ready now to love and serve others.

Love and service in little things

Does this love and compassion that flows from meditation always have to be expressed in great deeds of social action? Not really. That action can be a small, unselfish act by a young child. Jesus said, "Unless you change and become like a little child you will not enter the kingdom of Heaven" (Matthew 18:3). The following story by Macrina Wiederkehr in the book *A Tree Full of Angels* beautifully illustrates this truism and our need for childlikeness:

> One special moment of beauty that stands out in my mind I experienced in a bus station.... I witnessed a little girl helping her brother get a drink at the water fountain. Attempting to lift him to the proper height turned out to be impossible. I was just at the point of giving them some assistance when quick as lightning she darted over to a shoe-

shine man, pointed to a footstool he wasn't using, dragged it to the water fountain, and very gently lifted up her thirsty brother. It all happened so fast and it was so simple, yet it turned out to be a moment of beauty that became a prayer for me. So much to be learned from such a little moment. Perhaps what touched me most was her readiness to seek out a way to take care of the need without waiting to be rescued. It was a moment of beauty: a small child with a single heart.[32]

QUESTION 16

Q. What does the term "letting go" mean in the practice of meditation?

A. "Letting go" is an act of discernment and a description of a process we go through on the path of meditation. Not only do we try to let go of words, thoughts and images but also we try to let go of our concerns, fears and anxieties during our times of meditation. We even let go of trying to make the silence happen. It is also about letting go of the notion of getting anywhere. But letting go is also very much more than this. It is a complete self-surrender to God. It is called "letting go and letting God" (see Question 15 on measuring our spiritual progress in meditation).

We must also let go of desiring instant results in meditation. It has been said we live in an "instant results" society: we have instant coffee and same-day dry-cleaning service and can get information 24 hours a day on the Internet. Our society is accomplishment- and win-oriented. We are fixated on achieving goals, seeing immediate results and winning.[33]

The need to win

The Chinese spiritual philosopher Chuang Tzu (368–286 BC) saw the danger of results in his poem called "The Need to Win," translated by Thomas Merton:

When an archer is shooting for nothing
He has all his skill.
If he shoots for a brass buckle
He is already nervous.
If he shoots for a prize of gold
He goes blind
Or sees two targets –
He is out of his mind!

His skill has not changed. But the prize
Divides him. He cares.
He thinks more of winning
Than of shooting –
And the need to win
Drains him of power.[34]

Letting go of getting anywhere

This is why John Main keeps insisting on letting go of
expectations, of goals, of results and of "winning" on the
path of meditation.

A priest looking for results once went to John Main
and said, "I've been meditating now for seven years. How
long is it going to take me to come to any kind of silence?"
Father John, with a twinkle in his eye, said, "Twenty
years." The priest replied, "Just think, I have only 13 more
years to go!" The point of this story is that we must have
the faith of a child and give up our adult concern about
goals and about getting somewhere. Meditation is really
just the opposite. It is about letting go of our self-concerns,
and it's about letting go of getting anywhere.

Letting go of our attachments

Letting go is also freeing ourselves from our inordinate
attachments. We either let go of our attachments in the
silence of meditation or in death. But the great joy of the
meditator is that the process can begin before death, when
we begin to let go in our daily life and in our times of meditation – letting go of all the things we cling to, all our

attachments. We must let go of all our security, our attachment to health, material possessions, reputation, everything. We are going on a journey and we must travel light. This is perhaps what Jesus meant when he said to his disciples, "Take no gold, no silver, nor copper in your belts, no bag for your journey, nor two tunics, nor sandals, nor a staff" (Matthew 10:9-10).

St. John of the Cross had this to say about detachment and letting go.

> In order to have pleasure in everything
> Desire to have pleasure in nothing.
> In order to arrive at possessing everything
> Desire to possess nothing.
>
> In order to arrive at being everything
> Desire to be nothing.
>
> In order to arrive at knowing everything
> Desire to know nothing.[35]

Leaving my cares forgotten among the lilies

The point John of the Cross makes is that in God we possess all things, but in order to possess God we must give up all our inordinate desires. Once we do that, everything is given to us. Letting go frees us from all desires that are not centred in God. This is what John Cassian meant by non-possessiveness or "poverty of Spirit" (see Question 32 on John Cassian).

This letting go is also aptly expressed by St. John of the Cross in his poem "The Dark Night":

> I abandoned and forgot myself,
> Laying My Face on my Beloved;
> All things ceased; I went out from myself,
> Leaving my cares
> Forgotten among the lilies.[36]

John of the Cross had discovered that to love and to let go can be the same thing.

QUESTION 17

Q. Those who pray in a contemplative way speak of "the gift of tears." What exactly is this?

A. The gift of tears is a charism well known to the early desert monks, who saw it as a sign of a second baptism, not by water, but by the Holy Spirit. St. John Climacus comments on this: "Greater than Baptism itself is the fountain of tears after Baptism." This same saint adds, "Tears shed from fear intercede for us; but tears of all-holy love show us that our prayer has been accepted." Of interest to meditators is a saying of Isaac the Syrian, who commented that "after tears, comes the stilling of thoughts."

Compunction of heart

St. John Chrysostom emphasized that sorrow for our sins and compunction of heart (*Penthos*) is essential to the practice of any spirituality. This doctrine of penthos emphasizes the metanoia or conversion of heart that everyone must experience on the spiritual path. The gift of tears flows from compunction and is a meltdown of our heart of stone, which is then replaced by a heart of flesh. The prophet Ezekiel says:

> A new heart I will give you, and a new spirit I will put within you; I will take out of your flesh the heart of stone and give you a heart of flesh. And I will put my spirit within you...and you shall be my people, and I will be your God. (Ezekiel 36:27-28)

St. Evagrius of Pontus once said, "Before all else, pray to be given tears, that weeping may soften the savage hardness which is in your soul." The desert monk Abbot Pimen said: "Weep, there is no other way to perfection." Both St. Ignatius, founder of the Jesuits, and St. Benedict experienced the gift of tears, but throughout all the ages Christians in every walk of life have been at times filled with such a great tenderness and longing for God that they have wept with both sorrow and joy.

Weeping in our own brokenness

Weeping also seems to be an authentic experience and acknowledgement of our own brokenness and woundedness that leads us to inner healing. This acknowledgement of our own woundedness is echoed in St. Paul's cry:

> But I am unspiritual; I have been sold as a slave to sin. I cannot understand my own behaviour. I fail to carry out the things I want to do, and I find myself doing the very things I hate...and so the thing behaving in that way is not my self but sin living in me.... When I act against my will, then, it is not my true self doing it, but sin which lives in me.... What a wretched person I am! Who will rescue me from this body, doomed to death? Thanks be to God through Jesus Christ our Lord. (Romans 7:14-25)

A return to the true self

This lifelong spiritual battle with the ego – the false or illusory self that St. Paul hints at – is the process of *metanoia* or conversion of heart spoken of by the prophet Ezekiel. Metanoia is a return to the true self (see Question 29 on the true and false self).

Interior tears are a sure sign of compunction at the core of our being. The prophet Joel speaks of this conversion:

> Come back to me with all your heart,
> fasting, weeping, mourning.
> Let your hearts be broken, not your garments torn.
> Turn to the LORD, your God, again,
> for he is all tenderness and compassion,
> slow to anger, rich in graciousness,
> and ready to relent. (Joel 2:12-13)

Isaac the Syrian has described the gift of tears as a new birth that comes only after an inner conversion and a long purification. (For a modern reference to the gift of tears, see Question 38 on Etty Hillesum.)

Practical thoughts about tears

Now some practical thoughts about tears. As mentioned, tears indicate a warming of our heart. They may come at unexpected moments – during spiritual reading, participating in the Eucharist, even washing dishes. We cannot force the gift of tears. Like all charisms, it is a gift from God. We must be aware, however, that there can be neurotic tears, tears of grief and tears that flow from hysteria. The sign of the true gift of tears is an abiding inner peace, joy and love deep in one's heart.

QUESTION 18

Q. Is it necessary to meditate in a church or can one meditate anywhere?

A. Meister Eckhart, the great medieval spiritual teacher, says, "God is equally in all things and in all places." It is true that the presence of Christ takes many forms. He is present in the Eucharist under the form of bread and wine, but he is also present in the worshipping community, the Scriptures and where two or three are gathered in his name, for he says, "There I am in the midst of them" (Matthew 18:20). He is also present, as Matthew points out, in the hungry, the thirsty, the naked and those in prison: "Lord, when did we see you hungry and fed you or thirsty and gave you drink?" (Matthew 25:37) He is also present in our hearts at our times of meditation.

Where a person meditates is holy ground

As Eckhart says, when Christ is present, he is wholly present. He is not *more* present in the Blessed Sacrament and *less* present in the gathering of two or three of the worshipping community or in our hearts during medita-

tion. So for that reason, the place where a person meditates is holy ground, whether it is in a church, on a bus,
beside a river, in prison, in a garden or at home. John
Main pointed out in the book *The Present Christ*[37] that God
cannot be *more* or *less* present, as God is indivisible and
therefore cannot be divided into more or less.

QUESTION 19

Q. What is the "Gethsemani sleep" in meditation?

A. The "Gethsemani sleep" is all about attention in prayer.
There is a story about a Japanese Buddhist master who
was asked by a visiting foreign student to describe the
most important teaching about Buddhist meditation. The
teacher took a brush and wrote out the Japanese word for
"attention" and handed it to the visitor. Thinking this to be
too brief for a profound teaching, the student asked if he
would add something to it. The Buddhist teaching master
took his brush and wrote "attention, attention." When
pressed again by the student for something more, he
wrote with his brush, "attention, attention, attention."

"Could you not watch one hour with me?"

Certainly attention was what Jesus was asking his disciples for in the Garden of Gethsemani when he said to
them, "Wait here and watch with me." In Matthew's gospel
he said to his friends, "My soul is very sorrowful even to
death" (Matthew 26:38). And before going to pray, he
asked them to keep watch nearby. They tried, but fell
asleep. Jesus was asking them for a different spiritual discipline to stay awake and keep watch. "Could you not
watch one hour with me?" asked Jesus. "Watch and pray
that you may not enter into temptation. The Spirit is willing but the flesh is weak." (Matthew 26:40-42)

The call to wakefulness

In Gethsemani, we see Jesus in his most human hour, in
anguish and fear. When Jesus asked his disciples to keep

watch, he was not asking them to stand guard in order to warn him when Judas came. He was not about to run away. He was asking them to watch *with* him, to wait and be awake with him in his hour of crisis. Twice he asked them, and twice he returned to find them sleeping. If Jesus had asked them to flee with him or to rally support- ers, these three disciples would certainly have stayed awake and worked tirelessly through the whole night. But he was not calling them to heroic action; he was not ask- ing them to "do" anything at all. He was calling them to simple attention, to watchfulness, to be with him. As we see in the gospel, that was infinitely more difficult.

We are asked to *be* rather than *do*

How many of us still immerse ourselves in activity, rush- ing to and fro, busy, busy, busy because the call of Jesus to "keep watch and wait" seems too great a challenge? Yes, keeping watch is certainly one of the hardest things. And yet that is what the practice of meditation is all about: keeping watch. Gethsemani reminds us that what we are asked to do is something more simple and difficult than springing into action. We are asked to *be* rather than do, to simply keep watch and stay awake.

Buddha replied "I am awake"

In Mark's gospel, Jesus says, "Remain here and keep awake." (Mark 14:35) That's what we do in our daily med- itation. We remain with the Lord and stay awake. There is a story about Buddhism and wakefulness. A delegation was once sent to the Buddha and asked him, "Who are you? Are you a god?" Buddha replied, "I am not." "Are you an angel?" "I am not," replied the Buddha. "Are you a prophet?" they persisted. "No," Buddha replied. "Who are you, then?" they asked. Buddha replied, "I am awake."

This is what Christian Meditation is all about: staying awake. It's about answering Jesus' call to his disciples to watch one hour with him, to stay awake and be attentive.

In our daily hour of meditation we fulfill this request of Jesus. The continual repetition of our mantra helps us to be attentive, fully awake, and keeps us from falling into the "Gethsemani sleep."

Perhaps the psalmist summed it up best: "Wait for the LORD: be strong, and let your heart take courage; wait for the LORD" (Psalm 27:14).

QUESTION 20

Q. I'm a very busy parish priest with all sorts of daily commitments, obligations and responsibilities. How can I set aside an hour a day to meditate?

A. That reminds me of the desert monk who once said:

> Unless there is a *still* centre
> in the middle of the storm
> Unless a person in the midst of all their
> activities
> preserves a secret room in their heart
> where they stand alone before God,
> Unless we do this we will lose all sense of
> spiritual direction and be torn to pieces.[38]

And then there is that wonderful story by James Truslow in the book *The Tempo of Modern Life*:

> A friend of mine, a distinguished explorer who spent a couple of years among the savages of the Upper Amazon, once attempted a forced march through the jungle. The party made extraordinary speed for the first two days, but on the third morning, when it was time to start, my friend found all the natives sitting on their haunches, looking very solemn and making no preparation to leave.
>
> "They are waiting," the chief explained to my friend. "They cannot move further until their souls have caught up to their bodies."[39]

This is perhaps a reminder that all of us, not just priests, need to let our souls catch up to our bodies. In an age of frenetic activity there is a spiritual, psychological and psychosomatic need to slow down, to find time for the soul and reverse patterns of excessive busyness. Constant hurry and pressure – day in and day out – take their toll on our nervous system. Evelyn Underhill (see Question 40) once said, "A lot of the road to heaven has to be taken at 30 mph." Even God rested from great activity. Scripture says, "After all his work God rested" (Genesis 2:2, Hebrews 4:4). We also need to rest each day in God's loving, silent presence.

Being is more important than doing
The problem, of course, for many priests is that with fewer and fewer priests, feverish activity is becoming the norm. The possibility of burnout is more and more present. There is a temptation to stay on the treadmill of busyness and activity and put off the spiritual reality that *being* is more important than *doing*.

We convince ourselves that we have so much to do, that we have numerous responsibilities to others and that it is impossible to reverse our workaholic pattern of doing...doing...doing. It's a treadmill many priests feel they can't get off.

Thomas Merton and Mother Teresa on prayer and giving to others
But Thomas Merton, the great American Cistercian monk, has perhaps put busyness and serving others in its proper context. Says Merton, "It is in deep solitude and silence that I find the gentleness with which I can truly love my brother and sister." And Mother Teresa once said, "God is the friend of silence. See how nature, trees, flowers, grass, grow in silence. The more we receive in silent prayer, the more we can give in our active life."

Much of the time we run on tired cylinders. There's a truism that our powers of giving are fairly well used up by noon on most days. Contemplative prayer opens us up to the energy and power of the Spirit. Our capacity to keep giving all day long increases. One is able to adjust to difficult problems and even to live with impossible situations. Of course, words are meaningless unless one enters into the meditation experience itself. We have to jump in the river and get wet. We have to do it.

Meditators have 25-hour days

With the daily discipline of meditation, one is able to accomplish what needs to be done with much greater effectiveness and joy. There's a saying that meditators have 25-hour days. The hour we devote to silence and stillness in prayer is returned to us in the form of spiritual energy and vitality in our daily life.

Giving priority to the spiritual discipline

How do we fit two half-hours into each day? A mother of nine children tells this story. When she decided she wanted to meditate, she got up a half-hour earlier to fit in her morning meditation. The evening meditation was a greater challenge. However, she found a "magic" half-hour in mid-afternoon when six children were at school and three children were sleeping. This is the kind of commitment we all need. We must give absolute priority to the twice-daily times of meditation. We simply have to build this spiritual discipline into our daily life (see Question 49 on prayer and action). Once it is built into our daily lives, the practice of meditation will guarantee a fruitful ministry.

QUESTION 21

Q. Why is saying the mantra so difficult? I'm discouraged by my inability to pray this way. Is it really worth all the effort and hard work?

A. It is a universal experience that as we move from using words, thoughts and imagination in prayer to contemplative silence, a purification takes place. Commenting on prayer without words or images, St. John of the Cross says:

> God now leaves them in such darkness that they do not know which way to turn; they cannot advance a step...as they used to now that the sensory faculties (imagination, intellect, will) are engulfed in this night. He leaves them in such dryness that they fail not only to receive satisfaction and pleasure from their spiritual exercises and works, but also find these exercises distasteful and bitter. This usually happens to recollected *beginners* sooner than to others.[40]

Three of the great obstacles in beginning the practice of meditation are discouragement, feeling helpless to control this way of prayer, and the challenge of *surrender* and *letting go.* Let go and let God, as the saying goes.

Stillness: a quiet martyrdom

Some of the great saints, teachers and philosophers point out that coming to a state of stillness is a great challenge, even at times a quiet martyrdom.

Lao Tzu (570–490 BC), the great Chinese philosopher, once described how to handle distractions:

> I do my utmost to attain emptiness;
> I hold firmly to stillness.
> The myriad creatures all rise together
> And I watch them return
> The teeming creatures

All return to their separate roots.
Returning to one's roots is known as
stillness.[41]

Hard work, but on no account think of giving up

St. Gregory of Sinai (14th century) speaks of the effort and labour in this way of prayer; he says that one will be tempted to give up because of the continual pain in saying the mantra. But, he says, "Persevere persistently and with ardent longing seek the Lord in your heart." *The Cloud of Unknowing* says, "This way of prayer is hard work, very hard work indeed...but on no account think of giving up." A desert hermit, Abba Agatho, said, "There is no labour as great as praying to God. Prayer is a mighty conflict to one's last breath." You are not alone in finding the discipline of meditation a challenge!

The one who loses their life will find it

There is, however, a great paradox here. It is true that meditation is often a way of darkness, of unknowing, and that God sometimes seems to have disappeared and we can no longer sense his presence. But at the same time this is often coupled with joy, inner peace and a firm conviction that we will find God in our aridity and distractedness through faith in his presence. Although we are frustrated at times, we nevertheless feel a mysterious yet powerful attraction to the indwelling Christ. And from time to time God will reveal his presence to us in the darkness. This is the work of grace.

John Main pinpoints a good reason why the practice of meditation seems at times so difficult for us. He reminds us that Jesus says, "The one who finds their life will lose it, and the one who loses their life for my sake will find it" (Matthew 10:39). But as Father John points out, we often become spiritual materialists, seeking to accumulate grace, virtue and merit. We are taught that success and winning are important in life, not *losing.* But meditation is a call to abandonment of all desire, a dispossession, a surrender and, in a real sense, losing one's life for God.

Meditation: a leap of trust into the unknown

The key here is not to become over-anxious about what is happening on the journey. Meditation requires a leap of trust into the unknown. God has a plan for each one of us and a particular path to follow. He already has the path mapped out. We have to be content *not* to see the way ahead. We have to let go of controlling, of knowing where we are on the journey. This is part of the death of the ego. Nikos Kazantzakis describes this letting go: "God is fire and you must walk on it...dance on it. At that moment the fire will become cool water. But until you reach that point, what a struggle, my Lord, what agony!"

The habitual experience of dryness and endless distractions reminds us that the path of meditation is one of pure faith. In the Christian perspective this darkness and suffering will lead to light and life. The prophet Isaiah has given us encouragement when he says:

> Whoever walks in darkness
> And has no light shining for him
> let him trust in the name of the LORD
> let him lean on his God (Isaiah 50:10).

God is present in darkness as in light

St. Paul also reassures us: "You can trust God not to let you be tried beyond your strength, and with any trial he will give you a way out of it and the strength to bear it" (1 Corinthians 10:13).

God is as present in darkness as in light. He is just as near in times of desolation as in times of consolation. Every spiritual journey has difficulties and setbacks, but the struggle to overcome them and persevere is infinitely worthwhile. Trials and crosses can be baffling but are God's way of eliciting from us trust, abandonment and detachment on the spiritual journey. When we cry out in our weakness, we have the consoling words of Jesus to St. Paul: "My grace is sufficient for you, for my power is made perfect in weakness" (2 Corinthians 12:9).

John Main does give us hope, though, when he points out that the recitation of our mantra should become easier as we persevere on the journey. With time, the torrent of thoughts lessens and one enjoys a greater sense of calmness, stillness and inner peace. This transition is aptly depicted in the Russian spiritual classic *The Way of the Pilgrim.* At one point the Pilgrim is "saying" the mantra, but one day he suddenly discovers the prayer "says itself," and he hears it spontaneously arising and sounding within himself. (See Question 36 on *The Way of the Pilgrim.*)

But again, this sounding within may come only after a lifetime of commitment to the meditative pilgrimage. Silence is a gift of God and is not earned, nor is it the mechanical outcome of reciting our mantra.

One practical suggestion to help you handle discouragement on the path of meditation is to join a weekly meditation group (see Question 51 on the role of groups). In the group setting we meet fellow travellers, often suffering from the same discouragement, and we can obtain strength and hope from listening to others on the common pilgrimage. Meditation is a journey we should take with others.

QUESTION 22

Q. Can children meditate?

A. Sacred Heart Sister Madeleine Simon, founder of two Christian Meditation Centres in England and author of the book *Born Contemplative: Introducing Children to Christian Meditation,* is adamant that it is never too early to introduce children to the practice of meditation. In her book she points out that the first years of a child's life are the time to nurture the seeds of contemplation and a deep and lasting relationship with God. Says Sister Madeleine:

The form of meditation discussed in *Born Contemplative* is one in which the mind is kept in silence within the darkness of faith through the repetition of a prayer word or mantra. Adults tend to have questions and queries when coming to this form of prayer, but small children have no such problems. They take to it like ducks to water. They have not reached the stage of logical thought and are able, in their simplicity, to *catch and hold God by love.*[42]

Not only can they meditate, they need meditation

Sr. Madeleine goes on to say that not only *can* children meditate, they *need* meditation in their daily lives. She points out that the lives of children today contain stress, tension, competition, noise, and often excessive activity and over-stimulation. They need to balance their lives with inner stillness. Interestingly, parents and teachers observe that once children are encouraged to meditate, they come to love their daily quiet times.

Sister Madeleine also feels that children enjoy a place to just "be." Moreover, they seem to have less self-consciousness than adults and with their unquestioning faith are readily able to bring their external senses to inner calmness.

The role of parents

Many children meditate with their parents. Children are often influenced by simply seeing their parents meditating and witnessing the fruits of their parents' daily practice. This influence on children of parents who meditate can be incalculable. Small children will often peek into their parents' meditation room to see what their parents are up to. They will soon connect a mother and father who are more patient, cheerful and kind with their parents' daily practice of meditation.

There are varying opinions about the length of time children should meditate. Sister Madeleine suggests very young children can begin by spending a quiet time of a few minutes on the lap of a parent and then slip away. From the age of five, she suggests starting at about five minutes and increasing to eight to 10 minutes when they are ready for a longer period, regardless of age. She also points out that some five-year-olds can be quiet for more than five minutes, while some 10-year-olds can hardly cope with a full five minutes. A discerning parent is required here.

I once visited a teenage Christian Meditation group in Dublin, Ireland, where the leader had adopted a rule of thumb of one minute of meditation for each year of their lives. We meditated for 14 minutes with a group of 13-, 14- and 15-year-old boys and girls. Their leader gave them a choice of a number of mantras.

It has been said that the best time to start a child on the path of meditation is when the child is in the womb. We now know the fetus is alert and sensitive to its mother's emotional vibrations, whether these indicate anger, stress, calmness or stillness. A meditating mother passes her calming inner stillness in an intuitive way to her child. The benefits of introducing young children to meditation will become even more obvious in early adult years.

How to introduce children to meditation

In *Born Contemplative*, Sister Madeleine provides guidance in bringing children to meditation through developing their inborn sense of wonder and by introducing them to the Scriptures and the dramatization of Gospel stories. She gives an example of how a parent or teacher could recount the story found in three of the Gospels about Jesus asleep in the boat. A great storm arises, with a fierce wind and gigantic waves. The apostles are terrified, afraid the boat is going to swamp. They cry out to Jesus to save them. Jesus wakes and says, "Why are you frightened?" (Matthew 8:26). He says to the wind and waves, "Be calm." At this point the parent (or teacher) can say, "Now let us spend a few moments being calm and still, letting God be with us." Of course, as Sister Madeleine points out, it is also important to explain to children that Jesus was present in the biblical stories, and he is equally present within us now in spirit.

PART TWO

QUESTIONS ON THE TEACHING OF CHRISTIAN MEDITATION

QUESTION 23

Q. Is meditation really prayer? I thought prayer was about talking to God.

A. From the earliest days of Christianity, prayer was understood as going beyond words, thoughts and images and entering into the presence of the Spirit who dwells in our inner heart, who dwells there in love.

Evagrius of Pontus (345–399), an early Egyptian monk and teacher of John Cassian, popularized the teaching of these early Christian monks. He once gave this classic definition of Christian prayer, which has been handed down through the centuries:

> Prayer is raising the mind and heart to God *through the laying aside of thoughts.*[43]

Evagrius refers to these desert monks who strove to find a means to lay aside thoughts. From this practice of prayer came the desert teaching of repeating over and over a prayer phrase to bring the mind to quietness and stillness. (See Question 33 on John Cassian and the Jesus Prayer.)

Saints and spiritual teachers through the ages have echoed this need for inner stillness and silence in prayer and finding the Kingdom of God within. St. Augustine (354–430), in one of his most beautiful insights into this spiritual path, wrote:

> O beauty ever ancient, ever new
> Too late have I loved you
> I was outside and you were within me
> And I never found you until I found
> You within myself.[44]

Stand before God with the mind in the heart

Those early Christian desert monks discovered God's abiding presence within them in silent prayer through the repetition of a mantra, or what in their day they called a formula. St. Theophane the Recluse expressed this practice of prayer when he said, "The principal thing is to stand before Him unceasingly day and night...with the mind in the heart, for in this lies the essence of the matter."

This way of using a prayer phrase or mantra to quiet the mind and bring one to the "still point" is the great rediscovery of prayer that we see spreading all around the world today.

Psalm 116:9 says: "I will walk in the presence of the LORD in the land of the living." By becoming silent in this wordless and imageless prayer we deepen our awareness of God's presence in our lives and we acknowledge our complete dependence on God. It was in the silence of the desert that God spoke to Moses and it is in the depths of our own silence that God speaks his prayer within us. As John Main says, it is not so much my prayer that matters as the prayer of Jesus into which we are led.

Meditation leads to attention, to concentration, to silence, to God

If one were to define the practice of Christian Meditation, one could say it is a daily spiritual discipline that leads one to attention, to concentration, to silence, to God. So meditation is much more than another method of prayer. It is about pure faith. It is a surrender of one's whole being to God. However, it is more a question of what God does than what we do. Meditation is entering into the prayer of Jesus to the Father in the Spirit deep within us. As John Main says, we are swept along in this prayer of the Trinity. While in effect we are doing very little in meditation from our own willpower or resources, a deeper force within us is doing everything. The Spirit prays within us.

Finding God at the centre of our hearts

The experience of so many who have begun to meditate is that through meditation we can find that God is at the centre of our hearts and that our lives are transformed by that discovery, by that experience. St. John of the Cross

(1542–91) says, "God is the centre of my soul." Julian of Norwich (1342–1416) says, "God is the still point at my centre." Meditation is this daily pilgrimage to one's own centre and a way of living from this deep centre of one's being. In ages past, coming to an inner silence and still-ness in prayer was referred to as contemplative prayer. Today it is pursued by many who practice what we call meditation in the Christian tradition.

Meditation gives meaning, shape and purpose to everything we do, to everything we are

John Main is repeating in contemporary language this same teaching of the early Christian desert monks:

> Meditation is a way of coming to your own centre, coming to the foundation of your own being, and remaining there – still, silent, attentive. Meditation is in essence a way of learning to become awake, to be fully alive and be still. The way to that wakeful-ness is silence and stillness. This is quite a chal-lenge for people of our time, because most of us have very little experience of silence, and silence can be terribly threatening to people in the transis-torised culture that we live in. You have to get used to that silence. That is why the way of meditation is a way of learning to say a word interiorly in your heart.[45]

We do not know how to pray, but the Spirit prays within us

Through fidelity to this simple practice this prayer of the heart leads us into the prayer of Jesus Himself. In going beyond words and thoughts and resting in God we allow God to pray within us. This ties into St. Paul's hint of what prayer is all about when he says, "We do not know how to pray, but the Spirit prays within us" (Romans 8:26).

Why not be totally changed into fire?

Prayer is much more than talking to God. In fact, as John Main says, silent contemplative prayer is even more than a way of prayer; it is a way of life that heals, transforms and sets us on fire. A famous saying of an Egyptian desert monk echoes this symbol of God as fire:

> Abbot Lot came to Abbot Joseph and said: Father, according as I am able, I keep my little rule, and my little fast, my prayer, meditation and contemplative silence; and according as I am able I strive to cleanse my heart of thoughts; now what more should I do? The elder rose up in reply and stretched out his hands to heaven and his fingers became like ten lamps of fire. He said: Why not be totally changed into fire? [46]

QUESTION 24

Q. I have a simple question. *Why* should one meditate?

A. Frederick William Nietzsche once said, "The one who has a *why* to live can bear with almost any *how*."[47]

In the book *The Heart of Silence: Contemplative Prayer by Those Who Practice It*,[48] 60 meditators recount many different reasons why they have taken up the practice of meditation. There seem to be as many why's as there are meditators.

John Main and the "why" of meditation

When John Main was asked why people meditate, he said it's very difficult to determine what exactly makes a person *want* to meditate. This had puzzled him over the years. He added that there seem to be so many reasons why people start to meditate, then went on to say that for everyone the *why* of meditation is an invitation to journey deeply into their own heart where they find only God, only love.

We discover the *why* after we begin to meditate

I believe that we all get an invitation to this way of prayer. In the Gospel Jesus says, "You did not choose me, I chose you" (John 15:16). For most of us the experience of silence and stillness will teach us about the "why" of meditation. In other words, we discover the real *why* only after we have started to meditate.

However, there are many ways of looking at the "why" of meditation. For Christians, the worldwide hunger and thirst for silence in prayer is undoubtedly the work of the Spirit. Perhaps we Christians are finally coming to a deeper understanding that our finite minds cannot grasp the infinity of God. We are beginning to realize that theology, philosophy or any other form of knowledge only tell us things *about* God. They do not bring us into the *experience* of God.

God simply cannot be grasped or known by the senses. The senses are involved with the world of space and time, but God is beyond space and time. However, when words, images and ideas are abandoned in the silence of prayer, we come to a deep intuitive knowledge and love of God.

Our hearts are restless until they rest in Thee

Perhaps we are also beginning to better understand our great longing and need for God, our need to wait on God, to listen to God, to be open to God in the stillness. We are finally beginning to realize the wisdom of St. Augustine when he said, "You have made us for Yourself, O Lord, and our hearts are restless until they rest in Thee." It's interesting that we often refer to meditation as "resting in God."

When we meditate we go into that secret place, that still centre. Out of that stillness where we are turned towards God comes the life of the Spirit, where we are transformed into love. We Christians meditate to open ourselves to the birth of Christ within. Perhaps Meister

Eckhart said it best: "God's chief aim is giving birth. He is never content till he begets his Son in us."[49]

God plays upon us whatever melody he wishes

Why do we meditate? Because in meditation God is working deep in our soul. On this spiritual path God is cleansing our soul from our failings and imperfections, sanctifying us and increasing his divine life within us. He is doing it within us because we have left ourselves completely at his disposal, not getting in his way. We leave him completely free to do his work. We are like musical instruments and God is the musician. We are at God's disposal and God plays upon us whatever melody he wishes.

Another *why*: the fruits of prayer

Why else do we meditate? Because in meditation the fruits of prayer enter our life almost immediately, and if we persevere on the path of meditation, the love of God overflows in our life like a reservoir. These fruits of prayer, the "fruits of the Spirit" as St. Paul calls them, include "love, joy, peace, patience, kindness, generosity, faithfulness, gentleness, self-control" (Galatians 5:22-24). This love will overflow in our lives in a thousand ways. But John Main reminds us that we can become intoxicated by words. The only important thing is to enter daily into the experience itself in faithfulness and commitment.

"Come with me to a quiet place"

Another reason why so many Christians come to the practice of meditation is the excessively noisy, busy world we live in at the beginning of the 21st century.

Even Christ and the apostles got caught up in activity and busyness at times. In Mark's gospel (Mark 6:31) it is recorded that one day the apostles gathered around Jesus and reported to him all they had done and taught.

Then, because there were so many people coming and going, Mark says, "They did not even have a chance to eat." Jesus, observing the frenzied activity, said to the Twelve, "Come with me by yourselves to a quiet place." Mark continues that they went away by themselves in a boat to a solitary place.

How many times in the gospel does Jesus withdraw to pray in a solitary place? Mark says, "But the fame of him went abroad the more: and great multitudes came together to hear, and to be healed of their infirmities; and he returned into the desert and prayed." This is the perfect balance between prayer and action in the life of Jesus. This is another "why" of Christian Meditation: we need to withdraw each day from excessive noise and activity and find God in the solitary place of our own heart.

To hear the voice of God deep within us

Just as Jesus and the apostles were caught up in activity, we also often allow our lives to become too busy, too noisy. We live in an age of frenetic activity. Television and radio programs bombard us. We have wall-to-wall distractions. Anthropologists tell us we are cramming twice as much noise and activity into our lives as our ancestors did. We are losing the contemplative dimension of life, and we are paying a terrible price. Noise is drowning out the voice of God. That is also why we come to meditation – to once more hear the voice of God deep within us.

We join others on the common path

Finally, there's one more important "why" of meditation. American Ken Wilber is the author of 14 books on anthropology, spirituality, religion, psychotherapy and meditation. In one of his books, *Grace and Grit,* where he writes of the death of his wife from cancer, he makes a very insightful statement about meditation. He and his wife had both meditated from their younger days. He says:

> When you can find a truth that Hindus and Christians, Buddhists and Taoists and Sufis in Islam all agree on, then you have probably found some-

thing that is profoundly important. Something that tells you about universal truth and ultimate meaning, something that touches the very core of the human condition.[50]

He goes on to say that this truth, which we all share despite our differing beliefs, is the direct experience of the Spirit deep within us in the practice of meditation. He says, "meditation then is part of the universal Spiritual culture of all humankind." While doctrinal differences seem insurmountable between the world's religions, the one unifying practice that brings us all together is this path of meditation, of the inner silence of prayer.

QUESTION 25

Q. Why is silence important in our lives and in the practice of meditation?

A. Undoubtedly this has much to do with our contemporary world, the cybernetic age of speed and frenetic activity, where we are now bombarded with an information superhighway that in some countries provides 500 television channels. Add to this the raucous clamour of nonstop radio, advertising, an inundation of e-mail, subliminal electronic advertising and supersonic jets and we have overkill with excessive noise and activity.

Our society seems to be geared to business, productivity, speed, material success and noise. Thomas Merton succinctly commented on the noisy pandemonium of our age when he said, "I am up to my eyeballs in angst." To counteract this age of too many decibels, the way of silence and stillness in prayer speaks to us of a deep human need and a spiritual path that is rooted in the "inner desert" of the heart where the Spirit is waiting.

God comes to us in the silence

Great things seem to happen in silence. On that first Christmas Eve, Jesus came to Mary, to the world and to us in the silence and stillness of the night. The Divine Office within the octave of the nativity says, "While all things were in quiet silence and the night was in the midst of its course, Your almighty word, O LORD, leapt down from Your throne in heaven" (Wisdom 18:14-15). The most famous Christmas carol is "Silent Night." God still comes to us in the silence, says John Main, but he comes to us now in the silence of our daily times of meditation.

John of the Cross, in a letter to a Carmelite nun, once wrote: "Our most important task consists in remaining silent before this great God.... He understands only one language, that of silent love." This stillness was also aptly described in his poetry when he wrote:

One dark night,
fired with love's urgent longings
– oh the sheer grace! –
I went out unseen,
my house being now stilled.[51]

Love unites with a bond that does not require words

In the many times Jesus slipped away from the apostles, I believe he would have spent the night in silent communication with his Father. We even find a reflection of this in human love. Two people in love often prefer to sit silently side by side, because talking would only disturb their loving union. Words would only be an invasion of intimacy. Love unites with a bond that does not require words. That is what the practice of meditation is all about.

I heard an interesting story recently along these lines. A person visiting a friend in hospital was sitting in the waiting room. She noticed a man in a wheelchair in some pain with his wife sitting next to him. For a half-hour the couple never exchanged a word, just held hands and looked intently at each other. Once or twice the woman patted the man's face. The person watching said the feeling of love was so tangible in the room that she felt she was sharing in their silent communion. Their silent love, she said, was also joyful and portrayed the fullness of a human relationship. That's what spiritual silence is all about. Love does not necessarily require words, it often requires silence.

"Silence gives our Spirit room to breathe"

John Main revealed the depths of contemplative silence in many of his talks. He once said, "You discover in the silence that you are loved and that you are loveable. It is the discovery everyone must make in their lives if they are going to become fully themselves, fully human. Silence gives our Spirit room to breathe, room to be." Nor is this silence a value only in Christianity. It is found in all the spiritual paths of the world's great religions.

The Old Testament also talks about finding God in the silence. The psalmist says, "Be still and know that I am God" (Psalm 46:10). The prophet Zechariah says, "Be silent everyone in the presence of the LORD" (Zechariah 2:17).

Elijah heard God in the deep silence

And then there is the beautiful story of the prophet Elijah. God says to Elijah, "Go outside and stand on the mountain; the LORD will be passing by." A strong and heavy wind comes, but the LORD is not in the wind. Then there's a violent earthquake, but the LORD is not in the earthquake. Fire blazed up, but the LORD was not in the fire. Then came a gentle breeze and a still, small voice. Elijah heard God in the deep silence (1 Kings 19:11-13).

Psychologists, social scientists, poets, writers and saints through the centuries have all understood the need for inner silence in our lives. They describe silence as a many-faceted diamond. Each of the following quotations give us a deeper insight into this universal thirst for silence.

A saint ripens in silence.
Georges Bernanos (1888–1948)

The present state of the world and the whole of life is diseased. If I were a doctor and my advice asked I should reply: create silence. Bring people to silence. The word of God cannot be heard in the noisy world of today. Therefore create silence.
Soren Kierkegaard (1813–1855)

The old man replied: "If he is not edified by my silence, there is no hope that he will be edified by my words."
Thomas Merton (1915–1968), quoting from a Desert monk[52]

I listen and hear the silence
I listen and see the silence
I listen and taste the silence
I listen and smell the silence
I listen and embrace the silence
Twylah Nitsch

I can't get Galilee out of my head. To think he remained silent for thirty years. Such a Silence!
Jean Sulivan (1913–1980)[53]

In the morning, while it was still very dark, he got up and went out to a deserted place and there he prayed.
(Mark 1:35)

We need to recover an oasis of silence within the rhyme and reason of our active life, for it is in silence that we meet God face to face…. silence stands outside the world of profit and utility. It cannot be exploited for profit; you cannot get anything out of it. It is "unproductive," therefore it is

regarded as useless. Yet there is more help and
healing in silence than in all useful things.
Max Picard (1888–1965)[54]

The Father uttered one word;
that word is His Son.
And He utters Him for ever in everlasting silence;
and in silence the soul has to hear it.
St. John of the Cross (1542–1591)[55]

Let us, then, labor for an inward stillness –
An inward stillness and an inward healing;
That perfect silence where the
Lips and heart are still,
And we no longer entertain
Our own imperfect thoughts
And vain opinions,
But God alone speaks in us,
And we wait in singleness of heart,
That we may know His will,
And in the silence of our Spirit,
That we may do His will,
And do that only.
Henry Wadsworth Longfellow (1807–1882)[56]

Nothing is so like God as silence.
Meister Eckhart (1260–1327)[57]

Silence is something like an endangered species.
The experience of silence is now so rare that we
must guard it and treasure it.

Psychotherapist Gunilla Norris

It is in deep solitude and silence that I find the gentleness with which I can truly love my brother and
sister....silence is not absence; it is opportunity.
Silence is the condition and the doorway.

Thomas Merton

There is a time to keep silence, and a time to speak.
(Ecclesiastes 3:7)

If we really want to pray we must first learn to listen, for in the silence of the heart God speaks.
T.S. Eliot (1888–1965)

We need silence to be able to touch souls. The more we receive in silent prayer, the more we can give in our active life. God is a friend of silence. The essential thing is not what we say, but what God says through us.
Mother Teresa (1910–1997)[58]

Silence is the folding of the wings, of the intellect to open the door of the heart. Such silence is holy, a prayer beyond all prayers leading to the heights of contemplation.
Catherine de Hueck Doherty (1896–1985)[59]

I think what all of us have to learn is not so much that we have to create silence. The silence is there within us. What we have to do is to enter into it, to become silent, to become the silence. The purpose of meditation and the challenge of meditation is to allow ourselves to become silent enough to allow this interior silence to emerge. Silence is the language of the Spirit.
John Main (1926–1982)[60]

QUESTION 26

Q. Why is meditation called the prayer of the heart? How does the heart enter into meditation?

A. Perhaps the famous poet and writer Antoine de Saint-Exupery (1900–1944) said it best in *The Little Prince*:

> Speaking to
> the Little Prince
> about love and life,
> the Fox says:
> And now here
> is my secret,
> a very simple secret.
> It is only
> with the heart
> that one can see rightly:
> What is essential
> is invisible
> to the eye.[61]

The heart has also been defined as the deepest psychological ground of one's personality and the root and source of all one's own inner truth. It is in our heart that we are aware of ourselves and of God. Perhaps that is the deepest meaning of heart. In meditation we say God touches our heart or we seek God in the silence and stillness of our own heart. When we give someone our heart, we give ourselves completely. That is why we often call meditation the prayer of the heart, because we give ourselves completely to Christ in the deepest part of our spiritual being – our heart. Meditation is this place where we encounter God in the depths of our own heart.

The heart: a rich biblical concept

Heart is also a rich biblical concept. Ezekiel says hardness of heart is a sin, and that we need "contrite" hearts. St. Paul prays that "Christ may dwell in our hearts in love" (Ephesians 3:17). The heart in the Old Testament's

Semitic understanding of the word meant the deepest reaches of one's inner being where love is generated in self-sacrifice for the beloved. In the Old Testament the word "heart" occurs over a thousand times, such as in Jeremiah: "Deep within them I will plant my law, writing it on their hearts" (Jeremiah 3:33). In the New Testament Jesus often talks about the heart: "Blessed are the pure of heart" (Matthew 5:8); "Where your treasure is, there your heart will be" (Matthew 6:21); "For I am gentle and humble of heart" (Matthew 11:29).

The prayer of the heart

Meditation is often referred to as the "prayer of the heart." Perhaps the best definition of the heart is that it is the deep centre, the core of our being, the place of unity where body, mind and spirit are one. We often say we want to get to the heart of the matter. The heart is the centre of a person, the centre from which we relate to God and to others. St. John of the Cross says, "God is the centre of my soul." If we do something from our heart, we do it with our deepest feelings, from our very centre.

The heart is known as our inner being, the inner spiritual centre of our being where God lives. Scripture tells us the source of prayer is the heart. Heart also has to do with openness. When we say "have a heart" we mean be open to me, be kind, be receptive. When we are wholehearted we commit and give ourselves fully to someone or to a cause. When someone is stubborn or closed, we say that person is hard-hearted or cold-hearted. When we deal with a warm-hearted person we know we will be treated kindly, our sorrows and joys will be shared.

The heart as a "still point"

It was the desert fathers who introduced the term "prayer of the heart," which meant a total surrender to God when one had abandoned mental images of God and brought "the mind into the heart." This silent prayer tradition of the desert monks was defined as a "straining towards God" but with a deep understanding that ultimately prayer is the operation of the indwelling Trinity praying within us. These early monks saw the heart as a "still point" where we meet in silent self-surrender and self-giving to God.

Perhaps St. Augustine summed it up most succinctly:

O Lord, you have created us for yourself and our hearts are restless until they rest in thee.[62]

QUESTION 27

Q. John Main talks about meditation as a path of "pure faith." What does he mean by this?

A. As we begin the spiritual journey our prayer is usually expressed in words, thoughts and images. Later, some people may be drawn to discursive meditation, where one uses thinking and imagining to reflect on scenes from the Gospel (see Question 54 on discursive meditation). Out of this discursive prayer, many hear the call to the simplicity of contemplative prayer, where one uses a mantra or prayer word as an aid to inner silence and stillness, a silence filled with the presence of God. In other words, God calls us from self-created experiences to his deep inner presence.

God's presence is not always a *felt* presence. The practice of contemplative prayer can lead into the desert experience with an absence of consolations and a time of barrenness, dryness and struggle. (See Question 48 on the desert experience.) As one meditator recently put it, "God seems a billion light years away. I have no sense of his presence." The sense of presence and of joy we may have experienced at the beginning of our practice of meditation now turns to ashes.

A time of purification

This is where pure faith enters the picture. This is a time when we are invited to growth and a weaning away from sweetness in prayer to more solid food. In this time of purification we enter into the fire of love; it is a time when we require great faith. Why? Because this time is a time of dying and finding new life. It is a time of stripping away or purging and a time of detachment from "sensible" consolations. It's a time when we hang on for dear life on our dark path of meditation and a time when we do need the gift of faith. It can also be a time of great distractions in our daily practice of meditation.

On entering the fire

John Main speaks about entering this fire:

> The purification that leads to purity of heart, that leads to the presence within us, is a consuming fire; and meditation is entering that fire, the fire that burns away everything that is not real, that burns away everything that is not true, that burns away everything that is not loving. And we must not be afraid of the fire. We must have absolute confidence in the fire, for the fire is the fire of love. The fire is even more. This is the great mystery of our faith. It is the fire who is love.[63]

Finding peace and fulfillment in the dark night of aridity

Thomas Merton points out that the reason for the darkness and helplessness in this stage of the spiritual journey is that the light of God is shining directly on our souls in the daily practice of meditation. In the book *Thomas Merton's Dark Path*, William H. Shannon quotes Merton:

> This cloud of darkness is "a powerful, mysterious and yet simple attraction which holds the soul prisoner in this darkness." Although frustration is experienced, there is no desire to escape from the

darkness and return to an easier stage of the spiritual life that preceded entrance into the darkness. At the same time "there is a growing conviction that joy and peace and fulfillment are only to be found somewhere in this dark night of aridity and faith."

Then one day there is an illumination. The soul comes to realize that in this darkness it has truly found the living God. It is overwhelmed with the sense that He is present and that God's love surrounds the soul and absorbs it. The darkness does not cease to be darkness.... but the soul has been awakened.... it is being drawn towards union with Him.[64]

One dark night... my house now being stilled

What does one do in the emptiness and darkness? St. John of the Cross is quite clear about this. He says:

Like a blind man [we] must lean on dark *faith*, accept it for a guide and light, and rest on nothing of what [we] understand, feel or imagine.[65]

John of the Cross is telling us we must enter the silence and wait for God there. We surrender to the silence by leaving behind our plans, expectations, our fears and hopes. We meditate with fidelity in childlike confidence and faith that God has a plan for each one of us and leads us by a dark path to union with God.

QUESTION 28

Q. How does the practice of meditation relate to other ways of prayer?

A. We pray in different ways at different times in our lives. There are many different forms or ways of prayer. There is the prayer of petition or intercession, vocal prayer, liturgical prayer in the celebration of the Eucharist, the Divine Office (now called the Liturgy of the Hours), novenas, devotions, stations of the cross, the rosary, charismatic prayer, speaking in tongues, and the prayerful reading of scripture.

Some people find prayer in God's beauty in nature. Singing can be a form of prayer and then, of course, there is meditation, wordless, imageless contemplative prayer. In fact, everything in life can be a form of prayer: gardening, washing dishes, eating, showering, changing diapers. We do not have to restrict prayer to the traditional and official forms or practices.

Indeed, Isaac the Syrian, a sixth-century monk and bishop, once wrote:

> When the Spirit has come to reside in someone, that person cannot stop praying; for the Spirit prays without ceasing in them. No matter if they are asleep or awake, prayer is going on in their hearts all the time. They may be eating or drinking, they may be resting or working – the incense of silent prayer will ascend spontaneously from their heart.[66]

Meditation is not the only way of prayer

In a talk to Cistercian monks in 1976 at the monastery in Kentucky where Thomas Merton had lived, John Main emphasized that meditation was not the only way of prayer. However, he went on to say:

> As I understand it, all Christian prayer is a growing awareness of God in Jesus. And for that growing awareness we need to come to a state of undistraction, to a state of attention and concentration – that is, to a state of awareness. And as far as I have been able to determine in the limitations of my own life, the only way that I have been able to find to come to that quiet, to that undistractedness, to that concentration, is the way of the mantra.[67]

Petitionary prayer and meditation

In one of his talks John Main commented on petitionary prayer (see also Question 31 on petitionary prayer):

> Is there such a thing as petitionary prayer? Has it any value? Obviously there is such a thing as petitionary prayer. Jesus Himself tells us to seek so that we will find; and so that we will receive (Matthew 7:8). The more you meditate, the more you realize that all the petitions that we can think of are already contained in the prayer of Jesus.... In the time of meditation we cast all our cares, all our concerns, totally on Him, surrender them to His hands.[68]

All prayer converges on contemplation

It is important to note that one who begins to meditate does not have to give up other forms of prayer. Meditation does not preclude praying in any other way. What usually happens is that the daily spiritual discipline of meditation becomes a priority, although we continue to pray in other ways at various times on our own spiritual path.

However, the Jesuit spiritual teacher and author William Johnston says that sooner or later all ways of prayer must lead to that silence wherein one rests in the presence of God. "All forms of prayer," says Johnston in his book *Being in Love*, "converge finally on contemplative prayer. No matter where you begin, you end with contemplation."[69]

QUESTION 29

Q. John Main often talks about leaving the "ego" behind in meditation. I always thought our ego was important and gave us our unique identity. Will you explain what he means?

A. In his book *Word Made Flesh* John Main says:

In commonday language, the essence of meditation is to leave the ego behind. We are not trying to
see with the ego what is happening. Egovision is
limited by its own self-centredness. The eye with
which we see without limit is the eye that cannot
see itself. The paradox of meditation is that once
we give up trying to see and to possess, then we see
all and all things are ours.[70]

Our false self always wants to be at centre stage

The problems of the ego begin with terminology, depending on which psychological tradition you follow. To simpli-
fy definitions, the word "ego" comes from the Latin word
for "I." It is true that the ego is what gives us our individual
uniqueness and our identity. Our true self is made in the
image of God, in which every human being is created. The
ego is a mirror image of the true self.

Unfortunately, in all of us this mirror image can be
mistaken for reality and become a *false self* that develops
in *our* likeness rather than in the likeness of God. This is
where we get the term "egocentric." Many spiritual teachers, including John Main, equate this false self with the
term "ego" or "egoism." But we must always remember
that our ego in the initial stages of our life gives us our
uniqueness and identity. It is not bad in itself, but it can
become a point of illusion, self-seeking and self-aggrandizement.

Our false self wants to control every situation

The false self develops many masks to hide the true self.
Our false self always wants to be centre stage. The false
self wants to be served first and think of itself first. Others
come second. Our false self believes the world revolves
around *me.* It is always seeking control, power, adulation.
The false self wants to control every situation and manip-
ulate others.

Eknath Easwaran has put the false self of the ego in concrete terms:

> Management consultants advise their executive clients to establish priorities before they start to work. The ego creates priorities too. At the top of those legal-sized yellow pads it puts "to be taken care of." Below on the first line it puts "me." There follows a list of all its requirements, which take up most of the page.[71]

Smashing the mirror of our ego

John Main speaks about our false self and the need for "smashing the mirror" of our ego (false self). He says that when we are united to God "as our supreme power source" we break through the mirror of the "hyper-self-consciousness of egoism." According to John Main, the root of sin is this self-consciousness which is a mirror, as it were, between God and our self, reflecting only our image and not God's image, which is our true identity. This mirror must be smashed, says Father John, and meditation is the means of smashing it. This smashing is non-violent; it is the work of love. There is absolutely no doubt that on the spiritual path one must struggle for this detachment from egoism and self-will.

The ego: sufferings spread like wild grass

In commenting on the ego the Buddha said, "For those whom ego overcomes, sufferings spread like wild grass." The ego's drive for self-aggrandizement inevitably leads it away from God.

William Law (1686–1761), the English Anglican mystic, put it this way in his book *The Grounds of Reasons of Christian Regeneration*: "See here the whole truth in short. All sin, all death, damnation and hell is nothing else but this kingdom of self, or the various operations of self-love, self-esteem and self-seeing which separate the soul from God."[72]

Everything at risk to enter the kingdom

Swami Abhishiktananda (Henri le Saux) says in *The Man and His Teachings*:

> The fundamental step in salvation, or conversion, is taken at the level of the human heart, that is to say, at the deepest centre of our being. This conversion, this metanoia of the Gospel, is the abandoning of all self-centredness, of all egoism; it is a total turning back of the whole being to God. In other words it is to place oneself in the presence of the Saviour.[73]

In the same book he is also quoted as saying:

> Jesus Himself taught that a person has to abandon everything, to put everything at risk, if they are to enter the kingdom. The Gospel is essentially a renunciation of and an uprooting of the self, of the ego, leaving it behind and following in the footsteps of the Master. (See Question 37 on Abhishiktananda.)

God possesses the secret of my identity

The false self exists, but at the level of illusion. It has no ultimate reality. But we can all choose to drop the mask, the illusion of this false self, and achieve our true identity in God. The journey to our true self is the journey of meditation because in the deep silence of our meditation we acknowledge our dependence on Jesus. Thomas Merton says God possesses the secret of my identity and the only way to find this true identity is by losing the false self in him.

Our false self: shedding an old snake skin

In meditation our egoism or false self melts slowly away as the focus of attention shifts from self to God and then to others. Why does this happen? Because the saying of the mantra is an act of pure selflessness. Each time we say the mantra we renounce and leave behind our own thoughts, our own words, our own concerns, our own fears, our own anxieties. In losing these selfish possessions we begin to lose the false self. In this detachment that meditation requires, the mask – the phoney disguise – is stripped away to reveal where the true "I" has been hiding. Like a moth, our false self is drawn to the flame where it must die. It must be discarded, says Thomas Merton, like an old snake skin.

The ego and forgiveness

Meditation develops a spirit of forgiveness. Many spiritual writers point out that forgiveness is one of the primary ways to combat the ego. When we forgive others for insults, real or imagined, we undercut the emotional resentment of the ego. As author Ken Wilber points out in his book *Grace and Grit*, the fundamental mood of the ego is never to forgive, never to forget. Forgiveness undermines the very existence of the ego.

Meditation is taking the searchlight off ourselves

Meditation helps us to shed the false self because in fact it is about self-forgetfulness. As John Main says, it is about taking the searchlight off ourselves, it is about self-transcendence. Could this be what Jesus meant when he said, "If anyone wishes to follow me, they must leave self behind, take up their cross daily and follow me" (Matthew 16:24)?

The Chinese poet Li Po put it this way: "We meditate together, the mountain and me/ Until only the mountain remains."

Laurence Freeman, Director of the International Centre for Christian Medition in London, England, tells the story about a sculptor who carved a superb statue of an elephant. When asked how he had done it, the sculptor replied he had started with a block of granite and then simply chipped away at everything that was *not* the elephant. That is the work of meditation. Chipping away at our false self, so that our true self – the image and likeness of God – may appear. Gradually we are purified in meditation of this false self and discover that God is within us and that he is the ground of our being.

Of course the journey from the false self to the true self is not always a pleasant, easy journey. There can be hiccups along the way. We do not like to change, but God who is love transforms us. To change is to die. It has very much to do with the passage from St. John's gospel: "Truly I say to you, unless a grain of wheat falls into the earth and dies, it remains alone, but if it dies it bears much fruit" (John 12:24).

In meditation, something dies within us – our false self – but something new is born. In starting off on this path, we cling to what is familiar and dread the journey to what is unfamiliar. That is why Father John says meditation at times requires courage and in the final analysis is a path of pure faith.

Our true identity founded in selflessness

On the path of meditation, our true self is more and more revealed and the shadow of the false self slowly dissolves. In meditation the mask of the false self is peeled away from our face and we find ourselves totally humbled and dependent on God. As Thomas Merton says, the false self is the "smoke self" and will disappear like smoke up a chimney.

Through the discipline of daily meditation our true self is slowly revealed. When this happens we can cry out with St. Paul, "It is no longer I that lives, but Christ lives in me" (Galatians 2:20). Now the spiritual journey seriously begins. Having found our true self we can begin to really love. Now the dance begins. We have found our true identity in love and our true self is *selflessness.*[74]

QUESTION 30

Q. Why does John Main not use gender-free, inclusive language in his recorded talks?

A. One must realize that Father John recorded these talks between 1977 and 1982, before there was a general consciousness or sensitivity about the use of inclusive language.

However, it is interesting to note that John Main believed firmly in the equality of the sexes and, in fact, left his priesthood studies with the Canons Regular in Rome in 1950 precisely because of an anti-woman bias he found in clerical circles in Rome.

In her book *Reconciled Being*,[75] Mary McAleese, the President of the Republic of Ireland, comments on this interesting aspect of John Main's temperament and career and writes about his courage in the 1950s in fighting this widespread anti-woman attitude. She refers to his positive attitude to women in the book *John Main by Those Who Knew Him*,[76] saying, "Main had an astute insight of remarkable maturity and sensitivity, well ahead of his time."

John Main's attitude to women

In *John Main by Those Who Knew Him*, an Irish priest, Father Paul Bowe, describes the circumstances regarding John Main leaving the religious community of the Canons Regular in Rome in 1950 as well as his attitude towards women:

> Sometime towards the end of the academic year in 1950 he called in to see me at San Clemente.... To my great surprise he was not his usual good-humoured, sensible, balanced self. On the contrary he was very agitated and disturbed; there was no sign whatsoever of his sense of humour, or even of ordinary indignation. In fact his whole demeanour was quite out of character.

He went on to tell me that he was thinking of pulling out altogether…it emerged that he was desperately upset about the atmosphere of the international house of studies in which he was living…. Apparently to use a modern term it was anti-feminist; in fact as far as the priests involved, it was quite simply anti-woman.

According to John, 'women' were as far as priests were concerned, to be regarded as 'snares of the devil.' Given half a chance they would lead us seminarians and priests astray from our vocations…

John had his wartime experiences behind him and the maturity that goes with them, so one can imagine the effect the kind of tommyrot he was being exposed to was having on him. The strange thing about the whole business was that he had never mentioned anything like that to me before, even though we used to meet nearly every day. I could only conclude afterwards that it must have been festering away like a boil that needed to be lanced but never was.

Father Bowe goes on to say rather prophetically, "Is it too fanciful to suggest that in God's providence it was in Rome in 1950 that the cage was opened and the spirit of John Main was set free?"

QUESTION 31

Q. Is there a role for petitionary prayer in the life of someone who meditates?

A. Definitely yes! Petitionary or intercessory prayer is taught by Jesus frequently in the New Testament. In Matthew 21:22, Jesus teaches us to ask the Father anything in his name and it will be granted. In the "Our Father" we are taught to turn to our heavenly Father and ask for bread. In John 14:13 Jesus says, "Whatever you ask for in my name will be given to you." St. Paul, in the introductions to his letters, is always praying for others and constantly says, "I remember you in my prayers." Jesus reminded his disciples, "Ask and you will receive that your joy may be full" (John 16:24).

The Christian community has always prayed for special needs

In Luke 22:31-32, Jesus says, "Simon, Simon.... I have prayed for you that your faith may not fail." In the gospel of Matthew Jesus says: "Ask and it will be given to you; seek and you will find; knock and it will be opened to you" (7:7). Throughout the ages the Christian community has prayed for its special needs. This intercessory prayer, therefore, will always be an important part of our spiritual life. We also see the role of petitionary prayer in the celebration of the Eucharist, especially in the intentions of the prayers of the faithful. We pray in this way not only for our own needs but for the needs of others. The prayer of the faithful in the Eucharist is not so much to inform God of what we need, because God already knows our real needs. Petitionary prayer is rather for the good of those who hear the petitions. We are not so much addressing God as sharing our needs and concerns with the eucharistic community in the faith that God already knows and that God cares.

On trying to twist God's arm

One problem with petitionary prayer is that we can become more attached to God's gifts than to God. We can unconsciously try to twist God's arm into giving us things. The prayer of petition can thus become very self-centred. We can begin to see God as a Santa Claus who gives us good things, and never open ourselves to silence and stillness where the Spirit works freely in our soul and prays deeply within us.

Father Patrick Eastman, in the publication *Monos*, talks about these false images of God:

The first, I call the "911 God," the God who is only contacted in the case of dire emergency. The second is the "Santa Claus God." This is the God who is kind of a superior magic-man who will fulfil even our wildest dreams. Finally, there is the "Vending Machine God." This is the one I most frequently encounter among Christians. It revolves around the idea that if I make the right kind of promises, or say the right amount of novenas, or rosaries, or attend enough masses, then, when I push the button, my request will be granted. Along with this view I find an awful lot of people who are mad at God. I mean, what do you do when you have put your money in a vending machine, pressed the button and nothing happens? You kick the machine, and I find that there are a lot of people who are kicking God for the same reason.[77]

Babbling on in many words

There is another danger in over-doing the prayer of petition. At a retreat I participated in recently, one person reacted against the prayer of silence, saying she had 68 people with assorted aches and pains, a laundry list that she must bring before the Lord each day. She referred to this as "getting my prayers in." And yet Jesus makes it clear that babbling on in many words is counter-productive. In Matthew 6:7-8 he says: "In your prayers do not babble on as the pagans do, for they think that by using many words they will make themselves heard. Do not be like them. Your Father knows what you need before you ask him." God, all-knowing, all-seeing, knows our real needs much better than we know them ourselves. This means that all our petitions for ourselves and others can be brought silently before the Lord in an instant of recollection as we begin our times of silent meditation.

A meditator recently told me the story of a fellow meditator who had all her petitions written in a booklet which she placed beside her before meditating. She would pat the book and remind God that she wanted to include all these petitions in her prayer as she opened herself to the silence of contemplative prayer.

A starting point on the path of prayer

Father Henri le Saux (Abhishiktananda – see Question 37) felt that the prayer of petition was only a starting point on the pilgrimage of prayer. He once wrote:

> To bring before God our needs and the needs of those who are dear to us may be, of course, a useful starting point in the path of prayer. But to save such a prayer from turning into and remaining an endless self-centred conversation with oneself, it has to be purified and progressively drawn higher and higher. The prayer of petition should become, at least with time, not so much a way of "informing" God of what he knows better than we do, as an act of loving adoration of his supreme Majesty, a true act of supernatural hope and of complete surrender.[78]

A deeper way of praying than words

Certainly the practice of Christian Meditation is a simple, deeper way of praying than words; it is a coming to the silent awareness of the indwelling Christ who is our mediator, making all human needs known to the Father through his universal compassion. It is going beyond words, beyond babbling, and through faith coming into the presence of God. This coming to awareness is not something we *do* but something we *are*. And in the silence we find love at the very centre of our being and our lives are transformed by this experience and by this discovery.

PART THREE

QUESTIONS ABOUT THOSE WHO HAVE PRACTISED CONTEMPLATIVE PRAYER: PAST AND PRESENT

QUESTION 32

Q. It is my understanding that John Main felt indebted to a fourth-century Christian monk, John Cassian, for his teaching on prayer and the use of a mantra to bring one to inner stillness. Can you tell me more about Cassian?

A. Cassian's date of birth is unknown but it was probably around 365 AD in what is today Croatia, but at that time was a province of the Roman Empire in which both Greek and Latin were spoken. At an early age he left his native land to become a monk in a monastery in Bethlehem. After two years, along with another monk, Germanus, he received permission to visit Egypt, where he spent 12 years visiting various hermits and studying the lives of the desert monks. Twenty years later, when he was the abbot of a monastery in Marseilles, he recorded his memories, experiences and commentaries in two books: *Institutes* and *Conferences.*

Cassian's influence on St. Benedict

These writings of Cassian had a great influence in Christendom and especially on St. Benedict. Benedict closely modelled his rule on *Institutes* and urged that Cassian be read regularly in the monasteries of his rule. Abbot Cuthbert Butler (1858–1934) writes, "St. Benedict was familiar with Cassian's writings and was saturated with his thought and language in a greater measure than with any other, save only the Holy Scriptures."[79]

Cassian and St. Thomas Aquinas

It is said that Cassian's *Conferences* was one of two books St. Thomas Aquinas always kept on his desk, alongside the commentary of St. John Chrysostom on St. Matthew's Gospel. Cassian also had a special influence on the writings and teachings of St. Dominic, St. Ignatius, St. Teresa of Avila and St. Frances de Sales. In addition, Cassian's writings played an integral part in early Celtic and Irish spirituality. There is no doubt that Cassian is a master not only of the monastic life but also of the spirituality of the early church.

"A treatise on prayer that has never been surpassed"

Cassian recorded all that he had learned on prayer in his *Conferences IX* and *X*. Benedictine Cuthbert Butler refers to Cassian's Tenth Conference on prayer as "a treatise on prayer that has never been surpassed."[80] In this conference Cassian essentially refers to a contemplative tradition based on continuous prayer and emphasis on the indwelling presence of Christ. These early desert monks employed a "formula" of reciting a short biblical verse to come to an interior silence in prayer. Today we would equate the formula with a mantra. We are indebted today to Cassian and his monk companion, Germanus, for describing this prayer practice of the desert monks.

Abba Isaac and his pupils

In this Tenth Conference, Cassian gives a lengthy account of a conversation between Germanus and himself as pupils and a great spiritual leader in the desert, Abbot Isaac, as teacher.

On their first visit Abba Isaac told them that those who prayed must keep their minds in silence and stillness. On their second visit, having tried to pray in silence, Germanus put their problem to Isaac. They wanted to pray like this, he said, but they found that their minds went travelling far and wide, from one idea or image to another, from one distraction to another. Germanus said, "I believe this happens because we haven't got any point to focus on. We need something to stop the wandering of our thoughts."

On hearing this Isaac was happy. Such an insight, he said, showed that the two young men were halfway to the solution. "With God's guidance," he said, "I think it will be easy to bring you to the heart of true prayer." Then he taught them to pray by means of a mantra or prayer verse,

what Cassian called a "formula." He urged them to repeat
a verse of Psalm 69: "Come to my help, O God; LORD,
hurry to my rescue." He also urged them to say this verse
over and over until it became rooted in their very being.
They should go on repeating this verse, said Isaac, "until
it casts away the multiplicity of other thoughts." Restrict
yourself, said Isaac, to the poverty of this simple verse, and
reject all the abundant riches of thought and words. This
verse must always be in your heart. It was not until the
fifth century that a formula or mantra using the name of
Jesus became a widespread spiritual practice. (See
Question 34 on the Jesus Prayer.)

Isaac tied the poverty of this simple verse to the beati-
tude "Blessed are the poor in spirit, for theirs is the kingdom of God." Isaac also told Cassian and Germanus to
repeat this verse in both prosperity and adversity. This is
where John Main discovered the tradition of the continuous recitation of the mantra in our daily times of meditation.

The desert tradition and the mantra

It can be seen from the practice of the formula and later
the Jesus Prayer that the practice of Christian Meditation
came from the same spiritual roots and the same desert
tradition. The tradition of the formula, the Jesus Prayer
and the mantra "maranatha" came out of that same tradition of silent, unceasing prayer practised by the early
desert monks. All mantras are repeated to keep the mind
and heart attentive to God's presence. The Jesus Prayer is
centred in the heart. The early monks said, "We must
stand before God with the mind in the heart." John Main
also recommends that the mantra "maranatha" be sound-
ed and rooted in the heart. This practice lays stress on the
important involvement of the whole person: body, mind
and spirit.

The mantra leads to poverty of spirit

Cassian describes, in Christian terms and with scriptural support, a universal spiritual discipline that leads to unity and integration of all levels of consciousness. The continual recitation of the mantra roots the verse or word in the heart, thus gradually leading to the state of continuous prayer enjoyed by Christ (Luke 18:1) and by St. Paul (1 Thessalonians 5:17). By leaving behind what Cassian called "the riches of thought and imagination," the mantra leads to poverty of spirit, the condition of letting go, of radical non-possessiveness that applies eventually, not only to what we have or what we do but even to what we are: a reminder of the Lord's command to his disciples to "leave self behind" (Luke 9:23, 14:33).

Thanks to Cassian and the formula

In all aspects, with the exception of the mantra itself, the similarities between Cassian's formula, the Jesus Prayer and Christian Meditation are expressions of the deeper practice of prayer in the Christian tradition. John Main always felt indebted to Cassian for his teaching on prayer, so perhaps it is best to end by quoting Father John in his book *Letters from the Heart*:

> Throughout Christian history, men and women of prayer have fulfilled a special mission in bringing their contemporaries, and even succeeding generations, to the same enlightenment, the same rebirth in Spirit that Jesus preached.

> One of these teachers was John Cassian, in the fourth century, who has a claim to be one of the most influential teachers of the spiritual life in the West. His special importance as the teacher and inspirer of St. Benedict and so of the whole of Western monasticism, derives from the part he played in bringing the spiritual tradition of the East into the living experience of the West.[81]

QUESTION 33

Q. What is the link between John Cassian's prayer of the desert monks, the Jesus Prayer of Eastern spirituality, and the practice of Christian Meditation as taught by John Main? Could you also comment in more detail on the Jesus Prayer?

A. The Christian Egyptian desert monks of the fourth century sought God in prayer through the repetition of a formula (what we call a mantra) with the aim of unceasing prayer leading to inner silence and the indwelling presence of God. (See Question 32 on John Cassian.)

The choice of a sacred phrase

In the days of the desert monks there was a great deal of flexibility in the choice of a sacred phrase. Abbot Isaac suggested to Cassian the phrase "Come to my help, O God. Lord, hurry to my rescue." The name of Jesus was often used in short mantric phrases but seems to have had no special preference, and there was no desert spirituality specifically centred upon the name of Jesus.[82]

However, from the sixth century onwards, the practice of this way of prayer came to centre on the name of Jesus and, in the Eastern Orthodox tradition, on a set formula: "Jesus, son of God have mercy on me (a sinner)," or sometimes just "Lord Jesus, have mercy" or even the single word "Jesus."

The Jesus Prayer and maranatha are from the same source

In the twentieth century John Main went back to the desert tradition of Cassian and chose an alternative mantra to a biblical phrase with the name of Jesus. For Western head-centred people, suggested Father John, the word "Jesus" can immediately start us picturing Jesus, and limiting our relationship to him by merely *thinking* about Christ. This is why John Main recommended the mantra *maranatha* in Aramaic, a language that would not conjure up any thoughts or images. Maranatha means "Come, Lord Jesus." It should be noted that the Jesus Prayer mantra and Father John's mantra both spring from the same source, the spirituality of the fourth-century desert monks. Both mantras are repeated to keep the mind and heart attuned to God's presence.

J.D. Salinger's *Franny and Zooey*

Many people have become aware of the Jesus Prayer through J.D. Salinger's novel *Franny and Zooey* and through the Russian book *The Way of a Pilgrim*. (See Question 36 on *The Way of a Pilgrim*.)

Salinger's story concerns Franny, a modern co-ed who has become fed up with the excessive materialism of her boyfriend and of her generation. She picks up the Russian spiritual classic *The Way of a Pilgrim* which relates the story of a simple peasant who, upon the death of his wife and child, wanders throughout Russia reciting the Jesus Prayer: "Lord Jesus, son of God, have mercy on me, a sinner." She also reads from the *Philokalia*, an 18th-century collection of writings on the spirituality of the Jesus Prayer. Franny says to her brother Zooey:

> If you keep saying that prayer over and over again, you only have to do it with your lips at first – then eventually what happens is the prayer becomes self-active.... I don't know what, but something happens and the words get synchronized with the person's heartbeats and then you're actually praying without ceasing.[83]

Franny represents the growing number of people who seek Christ-consciousness through the simple repetition of a mantra in times of prayer.

There are numerous books and articles published on the Jesus Prayer; this way of prayer is particularly associated with the Eastern Orthodox tradition of spirituality and with the monks of Mount Athos, off the coast of Greece.

Kallistos Ware, a Bishop of the Greek Orthodox Church, has written beautifully about the Jesus Prayer; he echoes the teaching of John Main on the path of contemplative silence in prayer. Says Bishop Ware:

> To achieve silence is of all things the hardest and the most decisive in the art of prayer. Silence is not merely negative, a pause between words, a temporary cessation of speech, but properly understood it is highly positive; an attitude of attentive alertness, of vigilance, and above all of *listening*. The person who has attained inward stillness or silence, is par excellence the one who listens. One listens to the voice of prayer in one's own heart and understands that voice is not one's own but that of Another speaking within.[84]

God's grace is a free gift

Bishop Ware also reminds us of the famous saying of Bishop Theophane the Recluse (1815–1894) regarding the Jesus Prayer: "The principal thing is to stand before God with the mind in the heart and to go on standing before him unceasingly day and night until the end of life."[85] He also reminds us that "there is no mechanical technique, whether physical or mental, which can *compel* God to manifest His presence. His grace is conferred always as a free gift and cannot be gained automatically by any method of prayer" [author's italics].

The Bishop offers these prayer hints which also reflect John Main's teaching on this subject.

Kallistos Ware on prayer

- The purpose of prayer can be summarized in the phrase "become what you are." Listen to him who never ceases to speak within you; possess Him who even now possesses you. Such is God's message to anyone who wants to pray: "You would not seek me unless you had already found me" (Romans 10:20).

Let the prayer speak, more precisely let God speak

- "Prayer...is not something which I initiate but in which I share; it is not primarily something which I do but which God is doing within me" (Galatians 2:20). The path of inner prayer is indicated in St. John the Baptist's words about the Messiah: "He must increase, but I must decrease" (John 3:30). It is in this sense that to pray is to be silent. You yourself must be silent and let the prayer speak or, more precisely, let God speak.

- True inner prayer is to stop talking and to listen to the wordless voice of God within our heart; it is to cease doing things on our own and to enter into the action of God. Such strenuous prayer is never easy in the initial stages and is described by the Fathers as a hidden martyrdom.

To be present in the here and now

- To contemplate means, first of all, to be present where one is, to be *here* and *now*. But usually we find ourselves unable to restrain our minds from wandering at random over time and space. We recall the past, we anticipate the future, we plan what to do next. We lack the power to gather ourselves into the one place where we should be – *here* in the presence of God. Instead of fighting our thoughts directly, it is wiser to turn aside and fix our attention elsewhere. We should look to the Lord Jesus and entrust ourselves into His hands, laying before him our own powerlessness.

Thoughts keep filling our minds with ceaseless chatter

- Thoughts and images inevitably occur to us during prayer. We cannot stop their flow by a simple exertion of our will. It is of little or no value to say to ourselves, "stop thinking"; we might as well say, "stop breathing."

"The rational mind cannot rest idle," says St. Mark the Monk; thoughts keep filling it with ceaseless chatter, as in the dawn chorus of birds. But while we cannot make this chatter suddenly disappear, what we can do is detach ourselves from it by bending our ever-active mind with...the name of Jesus.

• According to Evagrius of Pontus, "Prayer is a laying aside of thoughts. A laying aside: not a savage conflict, not a furious repression, but a gentle yet persistent act of detachment.

To stand before God with the mind in the heart

It is not difficult to see how all the great teachers of silent prayer converge on their teaching. The Jesus Prayer is part of this great historical tradition and is joined with the present-day practice of Christian Meditation and other forms of contemplative prayer in leading so many contemporary Christians to "stand before God with the mind in the heart."

QUESTION 34

Q. John Main speaks about the importance of _The Cloud of Unknowing_, its teaching on contemplative prayer and, in particular, its emphasis on the use of a mantra to bring one to inner silence. Could you elaborate on _The Cloud_?

A. The spiritual classic _The Cloud of Unknowing_ was written by an anonymous author in the latter half of the 14th century in the central east midlands of England. He was a priest, perhaps an English country parson or a monk. _The Cloud_'s final paragraph reveals him as a priest dispensing "God's blessing and mine."

The book was widely read in the 14th century, judging by the number of manuscripts still available, but was not published in a modernized English version until 1912, by Evelyn Underhill (see Question 40 on Evelyn Underhill). Many of those who practice Christian Meditation feel it is almost as though it were written for the 21st century. It is finely attuned to human psychology, common sense, and even some humour.

Written in a time of upheaval and change

The surprising thing about this great work is that it was written in a time of such great upheaval and in a transitional era. Western Europe was in the throes of the Hundred Years War; the black plague was decimating every country it entered, including England; social unrest was prevalent in the English peasants' revolt; the pope was a captive in Avignon; religious heresy was beginning its influence and medieval Christendom was passing away.

In the midst of all this there was a great flowering of interest in contemplative prayer by teachers and writers such as Richard Rolle, Walter Hilton, Julian of Norwich (see Question 35 on Julian of Norwich) and the author of *The Cloud*. In many ways the latter part of the 14th century reminds us of our present age with its upheavals, unrest, our own versions of the plague, and our age of tremendous change and transition.

God hides in a cloud

The Cloud of Unknowing is important because we see continuity in the teaching on silent prayer from John Cassian (fourth century), *The Cloud of Unknowing* (fourteenth century) and John Main (twentieth century). All three teachers offer the same essential teaching, but couched in the language of their day.

The central theme of *The Cloud of Unknowing* is that God cannot be reached by the human intellect but only by a silent prayer of love that can pierce "the cloud of unknowing." The author of this book, who says that God hides in the cloud of unknowing, takes this image from the book of Exodus where the Israelites are led through the desert by a cloud by day and a pillar of fire by night. At the transfiguration God appears in a cloud and says, "This is my beloved son" (2 Peter 1:15-18). In addition, Psalm 97 says, "The LORD is King! Let the earth rejoice.... Clouds and thick darkness are all around him." And in the Book of Kings, Solomon says, "The LORD has chosen to dwell in the thick cloud" (Kings 8:1-7, 9-13).

The use of a mantra

The author of *The Cloud* talks very clearly about the recitation of a mantra that can be used to pierce this cloud of unknowing where God hides. He says, "We must pray in the height, depth, length and breadth of our spirit, not in many words but in a little word." And he urges us to set aside our thoughts, words and imagination and consign everything to what he calls the "cloud of forgetting." He says we must give up all our thoughts and ideas of God, for "God can be touched, embraced and loved, but never by thought." *The Cloud* says this about the use of a mantra in prayer:

> Take a short word, preferably of one syllable...the shorter the word the better. A word like God or love. Choose which you like, or perhaps some other, so long as it is of one syllable. And fix this word fast to your heart, so that it is always there come what may. This short word pierces heaven. This word is to be your shield and your spear, whether in peace or in war, with this word beat upon the cloud.

> Lift up your heart to God with humble love: desire God but not what you can get out of him. Don't think of anything so that nothing occupies your mind or will but only God. Try to forget all created things. Let them go and pay no attention to them. Do not give up but work away. When you begin you find only darkness and a cloud of unknowing. Reconcile yourself to wait in this darkness as long

as is necessary, but go on longing after him you love. Strike that thick cloud of unknowing with your word, that dart of longing love, and on no account think of giving up. You are to reach out with a naked intention directed towards God and him alone.[86]

Summary of *The Cloud*

Here are some other points the author of *The Cloud* makes about this prayer of repeating a short word, the prayer of seeking God in silence and stillness.

- He warns us that we should come to prayer with no expectations, not seeking to receive any special experiences, visions, to hear voices and so on. *The Cloud* says that essential union with God is beyond all experiences.

- *The Cloud* stresses that God does the primary work in this prayer. Our work, says the author, is to become silent, but even this cannot be done without the help of grace. To be silent in prayer, he says, far from being a mere technique, is in fact a distinct call from God.

Satan cannot enter this inner chamber of your heart

- Another point *The Cloud* makes is that we should not be carried away by superficial feelings of any kind, be they feelings of joy or sadness, elation or depression. The author says in this prayer we are to remain poised at a deep point of recollection and in the ground of our being. Even Satan, he says, cannot enter this inner chamber of our hearts in this prayer. In this silence we can only be open to the voice of the Spirit.

- *The Cloud* insists that by remaining silent in prayer we are, in fact, helping the whole human race. While we do not think explicitly of anybody, we are helping everybody.

The prayer of silence burns out the roots of sin

- *The Cloud* points out that this prayer burns out the roots of sin and performs a function that cannot be accomplished by fasting, self-denial or self-inflicted penances. This flame of love that burns in prayer penetrates to a level of the personality upon which those penances and practices have no effect.

- *The Cloud* even inserts a little bit of humour. Perhaps with tongue in cheek, the author says contemplative silence even changes one's appearance, giving serenity to one's demeanour, unifying the personality and making one attractive to others. He says, "Even those who are not highly endowed by nature are rendered beautiful by this prayer." (Unfortunately, he does not say anything about losing weight or wrinkles disappearing.)

- *The Cloud* also talks about the cost involved in this prayer. The author says, "It is hard work, very hard work indeed."

God is beyond anything we can imagine

- *The Cloud* says one must empty the mind of all images and thoughts and simply rest in darkness, in the darkness of the cloud of unknowing. The author says that out of this darkness of faith will come a stirring of ardent love. The purpose of emptying the mind of images and concepts, says *The Cloud,* is to make one capable of receiving God's gift of love. He emphasizes that human conceptual knowledge is totally inadequate and imperfect. God, he says, is beyond anything we can imagine.

Silent prayer: a normal development of the ordinary Christian life

- The author of *The Cloud* writes that this way of silent prayer is simplicity itself, and that even the most unlearned person can attain this silence. He says this spiritual discipline is uncomplicated, and simply a normal development of the ordinary Christian life. Two other great medieval spiritual teachers, Meister Eckhart (1260–1327) and Johannes Tauler (1300–1361), reflect a similar teaching that the heights of contemplative prayer are offered to ordinary people.

One can see the great influence *The Cloud of Unknowing* had on the prayer teaching of John Main. *The Cloud* is still one of the great spiritual classics of our time. It is available in a paperback edition with an introduction by the Jesuit William Johnston. Another recommended book is the *Mysticism of the Cloud of Unknowing* by the same William Johnston.[87]

QUESTION 35

Q. In the book *Silence and Stillness in Every Season: Daily Readings with John Main,* the entry of July 19 indicates that John Main was quite familiar with the teaching of the English medieval anchoress Julian of Norwich. I also understand John Main asked to hear readings by Julian as he lay dying. Can you tell me about Julian's life and what she had to say about this contemplative way of prayer?

A. Here is a little about Julian's life, although her biographical details are sparse. The dates of her birth and death are not certain, but probably would be close to 1342–1416.[88] She lived in a special anchorite cell attached to the parish church of St. Julian's in Norwich, which probably accounts for her name. Her contemplative cell was a small room built outside the church with a window that opened into the interior of the church, enabling her to participate in the Eucharist. Another window gave access to those seeking counsel: a listening ear or what in modern times we would call spiritual guidance.

Her writings also indicate that a disciplined life of silence and stillness in prayer were the basis for her deep spirituality. An anchoress was traditionally walled in to spend the rest of her life in prayer and contemplation. Scholars also point to Julian's lively prose writing and the fact that she is the first woman to have written a book in the English language. She was also well trained in Scripture, especially St. Paul, despite the fact that she describes herself as "an unlettered woman."

Julian's origins

It is remotely possible that she belonged to a community of Benedictine nuns at Carrow Priory, only a half-mile from Norwich. She may have gone to school there as a young girl and may have later become a teacher and perhaps a lay sister with the community. It is unlikely she was a full choir sister.[89] There are numerous references to the Benedictine Rule and to Gregory the Great's writings on St. Benedict in Julian's texts. However, she is not mentioned in any existing records of Carrow Priory and she never refers to any specific Benedictine community of sisters in her writings. In addition, the presence of her parish priest at her deathbed, rather than a Benedictine chaplain, could suggest that she was a laywoman at the time. Others speculate she was a laywoman because of her beautiful understanding of the motherhood of God; they think it is possible that she was a widow whose husband and children were killed by the black plague that swept through Norwich in 1361. Because of the lack of records we cannot be sure of Julian's origins.

The revelations of Divine Love

What we do know is that at the age of 30 years, in May 1373, she became gravely ill, possibly of the black plague, and was close to death. A parish priest was called to administer the last rites, and it is recorded that her mother closed her eyelids in anticipation of her imminent death. In this near-death state she experienced a series of 16 visions gazing at a crucifix held up by the priest. She subsequently wrote a *short text* about her unexpected recovery and what she called the "showings." For the following 20 years she prayed and savoured her experience of these showings, and eventually in 1393 wrote what we know as the *long text*. It is known today as the *Revelations of Divine Love* and contains 86 chapters.[90]

The warmth, closeness and tenderness of God

Why does Julian appeal to us today? One reason is that in her writings she brings refreshing optimism, new insights into the nature of God, particularly the warmth, closeness and tenderness of God. More importantly, Julian is one of the few medieval spiritual writers who states it to be absolutely impossible that God could ever be angry at us for, as she says, anger and friendship are two opposites. God, says Julian, is loving, gentle and kind, which is the opposite of angry. She states, "For I saw full surely that whenever our Lord appears, peace reigns and anger has no place. For I saw no whit of anger in God, in short or in long term." She goes on to say that God's love is compassionate and never wrathful.

Thomas Merton on Julian

So inspiring are her insights that Thomas Merton made this astonishing statement about her:

> Julian is without doubt one of the most wonderful of all Christian voices. She gets greater and greater in my eyes as I grow older and whereas in the old days I used to be crazy about St. John of the Cross, I would not exchange him for Julian if you gave me the world, and the Indies and all the Spanish mystics rolled up in one bundle. I think that Julian of Norwich is, with Newman, the greatest English theologian.[91]

A message of joyful optimism and hope

In Julian's 14th-century world of social unrest and the black plague, a world not unlike our own, she speaks of a God of tenderness, a God of compassion and love. As the Dominican priest Conrad Pepler has said, we need her message of joyful optimism and hope when "we are in danger of being crushed under a lethal pessimism."[92] God's love rings down through the centuries in her revelations when the Lord says to her, "All shall be well, and all shall be well, and all manner of things shall be well." Her revelations encompass a wide range of topics and portray an unquenchable optimism regarding God's power to bring good out of evil.

God is also our mother

The *Revelations of Divine Love* contains one of the clearest expositions in all of spiritual literature on the feminine aspect of God, and the notion that God is also our mother. In Chapter 52 Julian writes: "...God was rejoicing to be our Father; rejoicing too to be our Mother...." She also says specifically that Christ is "our Mother... our Brother and our Saviour" and again, "Jesus is our true mother in nature by our first creation and he is our true mother in grace by his taking on created nature."

She goes on to say that as "the mother can give her child to suck of her milk, so our precious Mother Jesus can feed us with himself and does most courteously and most tenderly with the blessed sacrament." And finally she adds, "As truly as God is our father, so just as truly is he our mother."[93]

In *Revelations of Divine Love* Julian unfolds a clear account of divine love, in which she states that God is our divine mother; that we were created in the image of God, to love; that our purpose in life is to enjoy all that God has made, and to enjoy God by growing in love.

The meaning of the visions

In Chapter 86 Julian summarizes what she had learned in her years of prayerfully discovering the meaning of the visions. She says: "What, do you wish to know your Lord's meaning in this thing? Know it well, *love* was his meaning. Who reveals it to you? *Love.* What did he reveal to you? *Love.* Why does he reveal it to you? For *love*" [author's italics].

John Main and Julian

In one of her revelations Julian says, "For in the human soul is God's true dwelling" and adds, "utterly at home he lives in us for ever." Again, she says, "God is the still point at my center." John Main picked up on this saying of Julian's and in one of his talks says, "Meditation is a daily pilgrimage to our own center."

Once, in a time of prayer, Julian heard these words of the Lord: "I am the foundation of your praying." These words were a great consolation to her in her practice of contemplative prayer. Is it any wonder that Polly Schofield, a meditator in Montreal who helped care for John Main in his final days, reminds us that Father John constantly asked to be read to from Julian's *Revelations* as he lay dying?

"All believing prayer is precious to me"

Finally, as one might expect, God speaks to Julian about desolation and helplessness in our daily life of prayer and the need for perseverance. She says:

Our prayer brings great joy and gladness to our Lord. He wants it and awaits it. By his grace he can make us as him in inward being as we are in outward form. This is his blessed will. So he says this: "Pray inwardly, even though you find no joy in it. For it does good, though you feel nothing, see nothing, yes, even though you think you cannot pray. For when you are dry and empty, sick and weak, your prayer pleases me, though there be little enough to please you. All believing prayer is precious to me."[94]

No wonder John Main loved Julian, studied her revelations, and chose to listen to her writing of optimism and hope as he approached death.

QUESTION 36

Q. I've heard that the Russian spiritual classic *The Way of a Pilgrim* speaks about the "prayer of the heart." Can you talk about this?

A. *The Way of a Pilgrim*, first published in 1884, tells the story of an anonymous Russian pilgrim who walks through Russia (and Siberia) reciting the Jesus Prayer. (See Question 33 on the Jesus Prayer.) He has lost his wife, his home and his material possessions, and he has a physical handicap that prevents him from earning a living. The prayer of the heart keeps him company through his many adventures and hardships as a wandering pilgrim.

Pray without ceasing

The story starts off when the pilgrim hears a reading in church from Thessalonians (5:17): "Pray without ceasing." Pondering how to pray without ceasing, he visits various churches and preachers, but no one is able to explain how to pray this way. Finally he meets a holy monk who introduces him to *The Philokalia* (The Love of Spiritual Beauty), a book on prayer written over a period of 11 centuries by the Fathers of the Eastern Orthodox Church.

The monk then teaches the pilgrim to recite the mantra "Lord Jesus Christ, have mercy on me" and to bring Jesus in Spirit from the mind to the heart. The monk predicts that eventually the mantra will say itself of its own accord. This indeed happens, when at one point on his journey the pilgrim discovers the prayer "says itself" and he hears it spontaneously arising and sounding within himself.

Sit down, alone and in silence

The monk (called a *Staret* in Russia), known for his holiness and experience in spiritual direction, reads to the pilgrim advice from Saint Symeon, the New Theologian:

> Sit down, alone and in silence. Lower your head, shut your eyes, breathe out gently and imagine yourself looking into your own heart. Carry...your thoughts from your head to your heart. As you breathe out, say 'Lord Jesus Christ, have mercy on me.' Say it moving your lips gently or simply say it in your mind. Try to put all other thoughts aside. Be calm, be patient, and repeat this process very frequently.[95]

The rest of the story tells of the pilgrim's wandering with his only possessions a copy of the Bible and *The Philokalia,* and contains many charming anecdotes, miraculous cures and conversions attributed to the recitation of the Jesus Prayer. A further book by the same author, *The Pilgrim Continues His Way*, recounts further travels in Russia and a trip to Jerusalem, again emphasizing the benefits of reciting the Jesus mantra in prayer.

...Leading it to union with God

Perhaps the best defence of this way of prayer comes when the anonymous author states:

> Many so called enlightened people regard the frequent offering of one and the same prayer as useless and even trifling, calling it mechanical and a thoughtless occupation of simple people. But unfortunately they do not know how this frequent service of the lips imperceptibly becomes a genuine appeal of the heart, sinks down into the inner life, becomes a delight, becomes as it were, natural to the soul, bringing to light and nourishment and leading it on to union with God.[96]

QUESTION 37

Q. Can you tell me about the French Benedictine priest Father Henri le Saux, who lived in India, practised meditation, and has much to say on the subject of silence in prayer? John Main quotes him in *Letters from the Heart* and recommended his book *Saccidananda: A Christian Approach to Advaitic Experience*.

A. Father Henri le Saux, later known as Swami Abhishiktananda, was born in Brittany, France, on August 30, 1910. At the age of 19 he entered a Benedictine monastery and was ordained a priest in 1935. In 1939, at the beginning of the Second World War, he was conscripted from his monastery and was taken prisoner in 1940 along with his whole regiment. He succeeded in escaping by hiding in a field of tall corn and subsequently rejoined his monastery.

"I have discovered a new melody"

The subjects of his earliest monastic writings and interests were the practice of silent meditation, Gregorian chant, the liturgy and the mystery of the Trinity. With regard to meditation, he wrote to his sister, a Benedictine nun, at this time, "You know I love Gregorian chant more than anything else, but now I have discovered a melody which is more perfect than any other melody; I lose myself in the silence of the OM" (traditional Indian meditation mantra).

A yearning for India

In 1934, at 24 years of age, he had a desire to start a contemplative monastery in India, but it was not until 1945 that his abbot gave him permission to contact another French priest in India, Father Jules Monachanin. Father Monachanin had already lived for some years in South India, where he led "a life devoted to the understanding and service of India, guided by a single desire; to incarnate Christianity in the ways of life, prayer and contemplative characteristic of Indian civilization."[97] Henri le Saux's contact with Monachanin led to permission to leave for India.

"The soul of India penetrated to the very depths of my own soul"

Father Henri reached India in August 1948 and was never again to leave his adopted country. In January 1949, six months after his arrival, both Le Saux and Monachanin visited Tiruvannanalai at the foot of the sacred mountain Arunachala. There they met one of India's greatest spiritual guides and sages, Ramana Maharshi. This was a turning point in Le Saux's life, and he was deeply influenced by the Indian swami. In his diary he wrote:

> My mind was carried off as if to an unknown world.... the invisible halo of this sage was received by something in me deeper than words. Unknown harmony awoke in my heart.... it was as if the very soul of India penetrated to the very depths of my own soul and held mysterious communion with it. It was a call which pierced through everything, rent it to pieces and opened a mighty abyss.... The ashram of Ramana helps me to understand the Gospel; there is in the Gospel much more than Christian piety has ever discovered.[98]

The founding of Shantivanum

In 1950, along with Jules Monachanin, Le Saux founded the Ashram of Saccidananda, also called Shantivanum ("forest of peace") on the banks of the sacred Kavery River in Tamil Nadu, Southern India. In 1968 Bede Griffiths was to take over the running of this ashram. (See Question 43 on Bede Griffiths.) Both Le Saux and Monachanin took on the simple dress, customs and lifestyle of India. They also both wore the saffron kavi of the Sannyasa, "the monk who has renounced all." Father Henri took on the name of Swami Abhishiktananda, translated as the "bliss of the anointed one" or "the bliss of Christ."

Towards the North of India

After the death of Father Monachanin in 1957, Abhishiktananda felt more and more drawn to Northern India, especially to the source of the sacred Ganges River in the Himalayas. During 1957 he spent seven months touring the area. He subsequently returned in the following years to meditate and spend time in a small hermitage and, after 1968, settled down to spend the last five years of his life there. During his life in India he gave retreats, conferences and seminars, met with Hindus for dialogue and was involved in discussions of ways to implement the spirit of the Second Vatican Council in India.

Also during this time (1948–73) he wrote many books, including the previously mentioned *Saccidananda: A Christian Approach to Advaita*; *Prayer*; *The Further Shore*; *The Secret of Arunachala*; *Hindu–Christian Meeting Point* and others, and kept up his daily diaries, later published as *Ascent to the Depth of the Heart*. In addition, his correspondence has now been published as *Swami Abhishiktananda: His Life Told Through His Letters*.[99]

The further shore

Two years before his death, Abhishiktananda came into contact with a young seminarian from France, Marc Chaduc; in 1971 Chaduc joined Abhishiktananda in India to become his disciple. Abhishiktananda gave himself unsparingly to training Chaduc in the sannyasa tradition, a tradition that Abhishiktananda felt was practised by the early desert monks of the fourth century. (See Questions 32 and 33 on John Cassian and the desert monks.)

On July 14, 1973, at the age of 63, while running to catch a bus in Rishikesh, Abhishiktananda suffered a massive heart attack and never recovered his health. He died on the evening of December 7 and was buried in the cemetery of the Divine Word Fathers in Indore. His gravestone reflects the simplicity of his life. It reads "Swami Abhishiktananda OSB, born 1910, ordained 1935, died December 7, 1973."

The great contribution of Swami Abhishiktananda's life to contemporary meditators is his invaluable teaching on silent meditation that so impressed John Main. From the fruit of his experience, a faith that was tested, deepened and enriched by the spiritual tradition of India, we have been given a deep understanding of contemplative practice.

A selection of readings by Abhishiktananda

- People are on the lookout for ideas, and I should like to make them feel that what they need is to keep silence. The Spirit only makes himself heard by those who humbly abide in silence.[100]

- The fundamental step in salvation, or conversion, is taken at the level of the human heart, that is to say, at the deepest centre of our being. This conversion, this metanoia of the Gospel, is the abandoning of all self-centredness, of all ego-ism; it is a total turning back of the whole being to God. In other words it is to place oneself in the presence of the Saviour.[101]

The Gospel is an uprooting...of the ego

- Jesus himself taught that a person has to abandon everything, to put everything at risk, if they are to enter the kingdom. The Gospel is essentially a renunciation of and an uprooting of the self, of the ego, leaving it behind and following in the footsteps of the Master.[102]

- In June 1952 Abhishiktananda noted in his journal: It is not a question of attaining to the knowledge of God or to the Presence of God, but of recognizing, realizing that this presence *Is*.[103]

- I abide in this secret place in the depth of my heart, there –
  where all alive before God I am,
  where all alone with God I am,
  where all alone from God I am,
  where alone is He who *Is*.[104]

The creche is just a sign

- December 1956. The joy of Christmas, you know, is not only the creche. The creche is just a sign. It is into the cave within the heart that we should go to hide ourselves, lose ourselves, forget ourselves. This is the true cave where Jesus is born in us, and being born in us makes us into himself. This cave is the bosom of the eternal Father, where the Word is born and comes to be from all eternity.

Live in this cave in the depth of your heart

- Our joy at Christmas, joy in the family, joy in worship, etc., all that is so little beside the true joy, the joy of Jesus awaking to being that night in Bethlehem, the joy of the divine Word awaking to being in the bosom of the Father in eternity! Live in this cave in the depth of your heart, that mystery into which India has penetrated so deeply.[105]

- It is not only monks or cloistered nuns who are called to live face to face with this Presence, the Presence of God. All the baptized, indeed every child of God who lives on earth, has his dwelling in the bosom of that glory. Each and every one is called to withdraw to the secret place of their heart.[106]

Silence is a simple listening to the Spirit

- The spiritual person is anxious to interweave their whole life of prayer with moments of silence; silence during work and routine occupations of the day; silence above all during meditation, whatever form it may take. This silence will first be silence of the tongue, then silence of useless thoughts and desires, and finally, silence of any thought, even of the highest. This last and highest silence is the one which has to be sought as often as possible during times assigned to special meditation or contemplation. This silence will be a simple listening to the Spirit within and without, a simple looking at the One who is present within and without, simply being attentive, being aware, being awake...[107]

Silence is the highest and truest praise to the Lord

• The aim of silent prayer is to quiet the mind, to free it from its instability and its innate tendency to dispersion, to gather it, as it were, at its very centre, to lead it, beyond all its activities, to the stillness of pure self-awareness. It is simply the preparation for the ultimate encounter with oneself, and for the ultimate encounter with the Father in the oneness of the Holy Spirit. Silence is the highest and truest praise to the Lord.[108]

QUESTION 38

Q. I have heard that a young Jewish woman, Etty Hillesum, who was killed at Auschwitz in 1943, practised meditation on her spiritual journey and is regarded as a Christian saint. Could you tell me more about her life?

A. Etty Hillesum did indeed meditate. In the book *An Interrupted Life: The Diaries of Etty Hillesum 1941–1943*, her entry for June 8, 1941 reads as follows:

SUNDAY MORNING, 9.30. I think that I'll do it anyway: I'll "turn inwards" for half an hour each morning before work, and listen to my inner voice. Lose myself. You could also call it meditation. I am still a bit wary of that word. But anyway, why not? A quiet half-hour within yourself. It's not enough just to move your arms and legs and all the other muscles about in the bathroom each morning. We are body and spirit. And half an hour of exercises combined with half an hour of meditation can set the tone for the whole day.

But it's not so simple, that sort of 'quiet hour.' It has to be learnt. A lot of unimportant inner litter and bits and pieces have to be swept out first. Even a small head can be piled high inside with irrelevant distractions. True, there may be edifying emotions and thoughts, too, but the clutter is ever present. So let this be the aim of the meditation: to turn one's innermost being into a vast empty plain, with none of that treacherous undergrowth to impede the view. So that something of God can enter you, and something of 'Love' too.[109]

Both Jews and Christians claim Etty as their own. Her story is one of the greatest personal spiritual testimonies to emerge from the 20th century.

Etty's story

Etty Hillesum, a 27-year-old Jewish woman and gifted writer, decided to write a diary during the German occupation of Holland. Into this diary she poured out her inner thoughts and feelings, which reveal the gradual transformation of an independent woman preoccupied with worldly pleasures into a vibrant person of great spiritual depth and wisdom. The diaries chronicle Etty's inner maturation of the Spirit.

In 1942 she voluntarily went to the German internment camp at Westerbork in Holland to serve those who were under arrest and detained. (Her correspondence, entitled *Letters from Westerbork*, was published in 1986.)[110] On Sept. 8, 1943, Etty and her entire family were transported to Auschwitz. A letter written by an eyewitness describes her final moments on Dutch soil. This person says that as she stepped up to and into the dark car of the cattle train, crowded with men, women and children, "She walked lightly, bearing the burden of these her people, yet caught in an inner calm. She had not been deserted by her God."

"We left the camp singing"

Another friend, who survived, saw her get on the train to Auschwitz and relates she was "talking happily, a kind word for everyone she met...full of sparkling humour. Then the shrill whistle when the train with a thousand victims moved out." She managed to throw a postcard out of the train, which a farmer found and mailed: "We left the camp singing," she said in the card. On November 30 of that year she died at Auschwitz.

Her friends treasured her memory; after the war they tried to find a publisher for her 400-page manuscript, which had been hidden for safekeeping. She had left careful plans for the survival of her diaries and letters, but was unaware that future generations would be able to read her testimony. It took many years to decipher her almost illegible handwriting.

Diaries published in 1981

Finally, her diaries were published in 1981. This extraordinary document of spiritual growth invariably revives readers' faith in humanity. Her diaries are now generally regarded as one of the great classics of our time and an authentic voice of the spiritual life. Next to Thomas Merton's *Seven Storey Mountain*, this is one of the most moving spiritual books I have ever read.

What do the diaries tell us? They begin on March 9, 1941, when Etty, a secular Jew, was living in Amsterdam and was going through a time of personal turmoil and emotional upheaval and feeling in need of psychotherapy. She consulted a psychologist, a Jewish refugee from Germany named Julius Spier. Under the influence of Carl Jung, Spier believed that human well-being and healing called for a spiritual dimension in one's life and that to be healed one needed the courage to say, "I believe in God."

From spirituality to social action

Etty fell in love with Spier and had an intense emotional and sexual relationship with him. In the process of their relationship she developed a religious sensibility that gave her daily diary entries an enormous spiritual dimension.

The word "God" appears often in her entries; she developed an intense dialogue with the divine. Her spiritual development did not lead her into a solitary withdrawal from life but rather into the thick of the world of action (see Question 49 on prayer and action). She threw herself into concern for social justice and service to the poor and oppressed; this continued until her death.

"There is a deep well inside me"

Etty soon felt the need to free herself from the obsessive attachment to Spier. Spier died suddenly in 1942 but Etty had already come to love the message more than the messenger. Eventually God became the most vital aspect of her life. In one of her diary entries she writes:

> There is a deep well inside me, and in it God dwells…. There are people who pray with their eyes turned to Heaven, they seek God outside themselves. And there are those who bow their heads and bury their faces in their hands. I think they seek God inside.

Etty was one of the latter, seeking God *inside*. She continues, "All that is left is the will to yield myself up to God…a desire to kneel down sometimes pulses through my body or rather my body seems made and meant for the act of kneeling."

The Jewish girl who loved Jesus

Some months before her death, Etty was speaking to an old friend who was a Communist activist: "a dogged old class fighter," as she describes him in her diary. She argued against the class struggle and then said, "I see no alternative: each of us must turn inward and destroy in oneself all that we think we ought to destroy in others and remember that every action of hate we add to this world makes it still more inhospitable." Her Communist friend was astonished and dismayed. "But that," he said, "is nothing but Christianity." Etty replied, "Yes, Christianity, and why not?"

Observers point out that Etty lived and died a Jew, but her insights into Jesus are deep and incisive and played a major role in her spiritual development.

Here are a few excerpts from Etty's diaries to whet your appetite. They may entice you to read what Canadian theologian Gregory Baum calls "rare documents of religious faith" that "reflect a deep level of mysticism."

Etty's insights on prayer and spirituality

- The misery here is quite terrible and yet, late at night when the day has slunk away into the depths behind me, I often walk with a spring in my step beside the barbed wire, and then time and again it soars straight from my heart. I can't help it, that's just the way it is, like some elemental force, the feeling that life is glorious and magnificent, and that one day we shall be building a whole new world. Against every new outrage and every fresh horror we shall put up one more piece of love and goodness, drawing strength from within ourselves. We may suffer, but we must not succumb.

"And I rest from time to time in prayer"

- But I refresh myself from day to day at the original source, life itself, and I rest from time to time in prayer. And what those who say, 'you live too intensely,' do not know, is that one can withdraw into prayer as into a convent cell and leave again with renewed strength and with peace regained.

- Truly, my life is a long listening to myself and, to others and to God. And if I say that I listen, it is really God who listens inside me, the most essential and the deepest in me listening to the most essential and deepest in others. God to God.

"In every human being I love something of You"

- And talking to you, God. Is that all right? I feel a growing need to speak to You alone. I love people so terribly, because in every human being I love something of You. And I seek You everywhere in them and often do find something of You.

- And I know for certain that there will be a continuity between the life I have led and the life about to begin. Because my life is increasingly an inner one and the outer setting matters less and less.

"There is a vast silence in me that continues to grow"

- I keep following my own inner voice even in this madhouse, with a hundred people chattering. There is a vast silence in me that continues to grow.

- That's how it went, more or less, my prayer this morning. I suddenly had to kneel down on the hard coconut matting in the bathroom and the tears poured down my face. And that prayer gave me enough strength for the rest of the day.

"There is a deep well inside me"

- There is a really deep well inside me. And in it dwells God. Sometimes I am there too. But more often stones and grit block the well, and God is buried beneath. Then He must be dug out again.

- One ought to be able to live without books, without anything. There will always be a small patch of sky above, and there will always be enough space to fold two hands in prayer.

All of life becomes one long stroll

- For once you have begun to walk with God, you need only keep on walking with Him and all of life becomes one long stroll.

- This much I know: you have to forget your own worries for the sake of others, for the sake of those whom you love. All the strength and love and faith in God which one possesses, and which have grown so miraculously in me of late, must be there for everyone who chances to cross my path and who needs it.

- I draw prayer round me like a dark protective wall, withdraw inside it as one might into a convent cell and then step outside again, calmer and stronger and more collected again.

The drop of water into the ocean of infinity

On November 30, 1943, Etty died in a swirl of Zyklon B gas at Auschwitz. The drop of water that had been Etty Hillesum fell into the ocean of infinity, returned to her God.

QUESTION 39

Q. John Main sometimes refers in his talks to the French writer Simone Weil. Can you tell me about her life? What does she say about the spiritual journey and the practice of contemplative prayer?

A. Simone Weil (1909–1943) was born of non-observant Jewish parents in Paris, France. In her teens she sympathized with pacifism, Marxism, the trade union movement and especially the working class. In her short lifetime she became a political activist, teacher, social critic, philosopher, writer and spiritual seeker.

Jesus and Charlie Chaplin

Concerned in 1934 with modern industrialism and the cult of production for its own sake, she took a year off from teaching to work in a Renault factory to understand better the pain of the conveyer belt and its detrimental effect upon the soul of workers. She once wrote, "Only Jesus and Charlie Chaplin understand the working class." (Her references to Chaplin relate to his portrayal of himself in his films as the "common man" and his identification with the underdog in society.) Weil joined in a non-combative role on the Republican side in the Spanish Civil War and ended her career working in London for the Free French during the Second World War.

A prophet of our times

In London she lived in great simplicity; she died in 1943 at 34 years of age because, although she was ill, she refused to eat more than the food rations her French compatriots were limited to eating in France. Very few people attended her funeral, and she was buried in Kent in a pauper's grave. However, since her death she has enjoyed a growing posthumous reputation as one of the most brilliant and original thinkers of 20th-century France. Many people regard her as a prophet in the purest Old Testament tradition.

Simone Weil devoted herself to a lifetime spiritual pilgrimage in search of truth and God. She said that her search for truth made her live "at the intersection of Christianity and all that is non-Christian." T.S. Eliot said that she lived her life "with a genius akin to that of the saints." From about 1935 until her death, she pursued a Christ-centred spiritual life of study and deep prayer.

To become one of His saints

Robert Coles, in his biography of Weil, entitled *Simone Weil: A Modern Pilgrimage*, writes:

> Once Simone Weil met Christ, her life began anew, a slave, now to a particular master. I think it is fair to say she fell in love with Jesus; that he became her beloved, that she kept him on her mind and in her heart. She spent the last five years of her life thinking about Jesus, writing about him, praying to him.... She was an ambitious, dedicated follower, anxious to meet him, maybe become one of his saints.[111]

Conversion experiences

Weil had three major religious conversion experiences: one in Assisi, Italy; one at Solesmes Benedictine monastery in France during Holy Week 1938; and one when she first read George Herbert's poem "Love Bade

Me Welcome." In savouring the poem she said, "Christ came down and took possession of me." She further explains in a letter, "In this sudden possession of me by Christ, neither my senses nor imagination had any part; I only felt in the midst of my suffering the presence of a love. God in his mercy had prevented me from reading the mystics so that it should be evident to me that I had not invented this absolutely unexpected contact."

"Love in the midst of affliction"

Her visit to Solesmes coincided with a severe migraine headache. She succeeded in attending a session of the Gregorian chant in spite of the pain and wrote:

> An extreme effort of attention enabled me to get outside this miserable flesh, leaving it to suffer by itself, heaped up in its corner, and to find a pure and perfect joy in the unspeakable beauty of the chanting and the words. This experience enabled me by analogy to understand better the possibility of loving the divine love in the midst of affliction.[112]

The experience of the beauty of Gregorian chant at Solesmes in the midst of suffering opened Weil to her deepest convictions that the cross is the central reality at all times and in all places. In her essay "The Love of God and Affliction" she wrote:

> The Trinity and the cross are the two poles of Christianity, the two essential truths: the first perfect joy; the second perfect affliction. It is necessary to know both the one and the other and their mysterious unity, but the human condition in this world places us infinitely far from the Trinity at the very foot of the cross. Our country is the cross.[113]

At Solesmes she had realized through experience "the possibility of loving divine love in the midst of affliction," and she came to understand, to appreciate and perhaps even to share the passion of Christ more and more.

On the brink of baptism

In spite of the fact she was powerfully attracted to the Catholic Church and even had a spiritual director in a blind Dominican priest, Father Jean-Marie Perrin, she was never received into the Church. She seemed to hover on the brink of baptism most of her life. She loved the Catholic faith but the authoritarianism of the institutional Church was quite another matter. Many observers feel she had the "Baptism of Desire" because she was already a Christian. She once wrote, "I love God, Christ, and the Catholic faith, but I have not the slightest love for the (institutional) church."

In the same pew with Thomas Merton?

When it became clear that the Nazi occupation of France would endanger the lives of Jews, Simone Weil and her parents fled to Casablanca in North Africa and then in 1942 to the United States. During this time she attended Mass at Corpus Christi church near Columbia University in New York City. Observers have pointed out that this is the same church to which Thomas Merton belonged at this time; it is ironic that two of the most influential spiritual writers of our times might have been sitting in the same pew without knowing each other.

Prayer consists of attention

Weil's voluminous writings on the spiritual life and prayer seem to have had an effect on John Main's teaching. Time and time again she encourages us to pray from where we are, not from where we would like to be. Her book *Waiting on God*, composed of letters to her spiritual director, Father Perrin, reveals her deep insights about silence in prayer and the need for attention and avoiding the Gethsemani sleep in our prayer (see Question 19 on the Gethsemani Sleep). In *Waiting on God* she writes:

> Prayer consists of attention. It is the orientation of all the attention of which the soul is capable toward

God. The quality of the attention counts for much.... Warmth of heart cannot make up for it. The highest part of the attention only makes contact with God when prayer is intense and pure enough.... There are degrees of silence. There is a silence in the beauty of the universe which is like a noise when compared with the silence of God.[114]

One day the soul belongs to God

Finally, in a very beautiful piece on prayer, Simone Weil writes:

From the infinity of space and time the infinite...love of God comes to court us. He comes at his own time. We can only choose to accept and welcome him or to reject him. If we are willing, God plants a little seed in us and goes away. From that moment God has nothing more to do, nor we either, except to wait. we must only never regret saying yes to him, our nuptial yes.

This is not as simple as it sounds, because the growth of the seed within us is painful. Indeed in order to allow it to grow, we cannot but destroy whatever puts obstacles in its way; that is, pluck up the undergrowth and the weeds...the gardening to be done has to be violent. Still the seed, independent of the gardening, does grow by itself. One day the time will come when the soul belongs to God.[115]

Hurrying home to be with Jesus

In the last paragraph of his biography, Robert Coles writes about the death of Simone Weil:

She looked upward, affirmed unflinchingly her last hope, the hope of heaven – and died, one suspects, glad at last, glad to be hurrying home, to be with God...with Jesus.[116]

QUESTION 40

Q. Many people feel that the great spiritual writer, scholar and teacher Evelyn Underhill paved the way for the renewal of contemplative prayer in the 1970s by John Main and other teachers of prayer. Could you comment and tell us a little about her life?

A. There is no doubt that Evelyn Underhill (1875–1941) was one of the most widely respected authors and teachers of prayer and the spiritual life in the first 50 years of the 20th century. Today she is recognized as one of the few voices in this period to bring contemplative prayer and spirituality from the cloistered life of the monastery and academic treatises to the everyday lives of ordinary people. In this respect she indeed served as a beacon and guide and gave impetus to John Main and others in the later years of the century. She is widely regarded today as a bridge between her spiritual times and ours, and as the principal spokesperson on contemplative prayer for her generation.

Her early life

Evelyn Underhill was born on December 6, 1875, in Wolverhampton, England, of well-to-do parents. The family placed no particular emphasis on religion, although she was baptized as an Anglican. Her childhood was comfortable and happy and included travel abroad. She attended Kings College, London. Later, in 1938, she received an honorary Doctor of Divinity from Aberdeen University.

A voracious reader, especially of medieval saints and the mystical life, Underhill, at the age of 32, seriously considered becoming a Roman Catholic. She put this off because of her fiancé's opposition as well as the subsequent condemnation of modernism by the Vatican, which she could not accept. Only many years later did she become a committed Anglican, into which church she had been baptized and confirmed.

Marriage and life in Kensington, London

Evelyn married Hubert Stuart Moore, a barrister, in 1932, and for most of their lives lived at 50 Campden Hill Square in the Kensington area of London, not far from the Christian Meditation Centre which, for a number of years, was located on Campden Hill Rd. I have made a number of pilgrimages to her home over the years; a historical plaque bears this inscription: "Evelyn Underhill, 1875–1941, Christian philosopher and teacher lived here."

A teacher of contemplative prayer

Over the years Evelyn Underhill wrote or edited 39 major books on mystical theology and spirituality, produced over 400 book reviews and articles, was in great demand as a retreat giver and lecturer and became a leading Christian teacher of contemplative prayer. She conducted retreats for 10 years at Pleshy Retreat House in Chelmsford, Essex. Her interests also included Eastern religions, and she had deep respect for the psychological aspects of the spiritual pilgrimage. In her personal life she enjoyed travel, gardening and sailing.

In 1911 she published a historical and analytical account of the mystical spiritual life entitled *Mysticism*,[117] which has become a 20th-century religious classic and continues to be published in numerous editions. Material for the book was drawn from the desert monks, Teresa of Avila, John of the Cross, Julian of Norwich, Meister Eckhart, Walter Hilton, *The Cloud of Unknowing*, William Blake, Jacques Maritain, and a host of others.

World War I and Baron Von Hugel

During World War I, Underhill worked in British Naval Intelligence but was not a militarist; her war experiences resulted in her becoming a committed pacifist for the rest of her life. Pacifism, she felt, was simply the logical and specific application of what she termed "the universal law of charity."

In 1921 she sought spiritual direction from a lay Roman Catholic theologian, Baron Friedrich von Hugel; he served as her spiritual director until his death in 1925. Her friends included two well-known Benedictine monks: Abbot John Chapman (1865–1933) and Cuthbert Butler (1858–1934).

"Prayer is a humble surrender"

Underhill tried to demythologize prayer and teach it in terms of both psychology and grace. "Prayer," she said, "was not a willed struggle but a humble surrender." She also stated that "prayer is caught, not taught." And she once said, "A lot of the road to heaven has to be taken at 30 mph."

Evelyn Underhill loved sailing and the outdoors, and often related the life of prayer to the life of nature, as in the following excerpt from a talk she delivered in 1930:

> Nothing in all nature is so lovely and so vigorous, so perfectly at home in its environment, as a fish in the sea. Its surroundings give to it a beauty, quality, and power which is not its own. We take it out, and at once a poor, limp, dull thing, fit for nothing, is gasping away its life. So the soul sunk in God, living the life of prayer, is supported, filled, transformed in beauty, by a vitality and a power which are not its own.[118]

"Be supple in his hands"

She gave this advice to a worried friend:

> Don't strain after more light than you've got yet; just wait quietly. God holds you when you cannot hold him, and when the time comes to jump he will see to it that you jump – and you will find you are not frightened then. But probably that is a long way ahead still. So just be supple in his hands and let him mold you (as he is doing) for his own purposes, responding with very simple acts of trust and love.[119]

The serene quiet within

Another of Evelyn's gems is this poem:

> It is God's will for us that
>   we should possess
>   an Interior Castle,
> against which the storms of
> life may beat without being
>   able to disturb
> the serene quiet within.[120]

Evelyn Underhill is indeed a great transitional figure of the 20th century. She saw all life as infused with the Spirit, and her legacy on the teaching of contemplative prayer and the inner life have been passed on not only to John Main but to all of us who can profit from her gifts of understanding, knowledge and love.

QUESTION 41

Q. Thomas Merton, the great American Cistercian monk, seems to have prepared the way for the teaching of John Main on contemplative prayer. Did they ever meet? How does Merton's life relate to John Main?

A. Thomas Merton was born of an American mother and a New Zealand artist father in the town of Prades near the French–Spanish border on January 31, 1915. A younger brother, John Paul, was born three years later. (In 1941, during the Second World War, John Paul joined the Royal Canadian Air Force and was killed in action over Germany in 1943.)

Their mother died when Merton was 6 years old and the boys were raised by their father, godfather and American relatives. He learned French, attended school in France and England, travelled widely and, in the 1930s, attended Cambridge University in England and then Columbia University in New York City. His father died when Merton was 15.

In the summer of 1941 Merton worked as a volunteer in Harlem at Friendship House, founded by the Baroness Catherine De Hueck Doherty, whose community of laypeople and priests, called Madonna House, still continues, a two-hour drive northwest of Ottawa in Combermere, Ontario.

On December 15, 1941, at the age of 27, Merton made the decision that was to change his life forever. He entered the Cistercian monastery of Gethsemani in Kentucky. (Cistercians are also known as Trappists.) In 1947 his famous autobiography, *The Seven Storey Mountain*, was published and has become an all-time religious bestseller with over a million copies sold.

Merton's groundwork for John Main's teaching

During his 27 years as a monk, Merton became an eloquent spiritual writer on contemplative prayer and has had a tremendous literary, social and spiritual impact on the 20th century, which continues to this day. In the 1960s he became a hermit on the property of his monastic religious community; by the time he died he had written some 60 books of prose and poetry. There have been over a hundred books published on Merton since his death.

It is no exaggeration to say that contemplation was the explicit theme of everything Merton wrote. We must give Merton much credit for the explosion of interest in contemplative prayer in our day. In many respects, Merton laid the groundwork for John Main's great success in handing on the tradition of contemplative prayer from the 1970s to the present day.

Merton was deeply serious about silence and stillness in prayer and the contemplative life as well as about social issues of his day, including the Vietnam war, the nuclear arms build-up and racism. He died of accidental electrocution on December 7, 1968, at the age of 53, after delivering a talk at a religious conference in Bangkok, Thailand.

Merton's personal influence on John Main

John Main and Thomas Merton never met. But in November 1976, eight years after Merton's death, Main was invited to address Merton's Cistercian community at Gethsemani Abbey on the subject of Christian Meditation/contemplative prayer. John Main's public teaching on meditation began in the three now famous conferences given to the monks and published as *Christian Meditation: The Gethsemani Talks*. But it was in the silent period spent in Thomas Merton's hermitage that the Spirit moved deeply in Main's heart and called him to the work of teaching meditation. John Main wrote a letter from the hermitage on November 13, 1976, to a close friend, Lady Lovat:

> I hope you are well. I am staying in Merton's hermitage out in the woods beyond Gethsemani. It is quite extraordinary how solitude brings everyone so close. I have just celebrated the most loving mass of my life in Merton's little chapel. You were all very close to me as I prayed for you and all your family.... My purpose in coming here was to talk to the community about prayer, but in fact I have learnt so much myself while I have been here.[121]

He told the monks at Gethsemani:

> ...As I understand it, all Christian prayer is a growing awareness of God in Jesus and for that growing awareness we need to come to a state of undistraction, to a state of attention and concentration – that is, to a state of awareness. And as far as I have been able to determine in the limitations of my own life, the only way that I have been able to find to come to that quiet, to that undistractedness, to that concentration, is the way of the mantra.[122]

Merton had blazed a path to the East

In his biography of John Main, *In the Stillness Dancing*, Neil McKenty comments:

> Is it any wonder Father John was so moved by his experience there? He knew Thomas Merton had done so much, in his life and in his writings, to make so many people think about contemplative prayer, so many people want to pray. Father John also knew that Merton, more than any other, had blazed a path to the East, a path that had helped John Main's own pilgrimage. There can be little doubt that, when Father John stood in silence at the altar of Merton's hermitage, he understood the other pilgrim who had arrived with the Master. And the experience of talking with the monks at Gethsemani became a turning point for John Main. It offered him a compelling motive to pursue his own journey, to clarify his own teaching on contemplative prayer and to speak about it to anyone who wanted to listen.[123]

Gregory Ryan on Merton and Main

Other authors have remarked on the key role played by both Merton and Main in the contemporary revival of Christian prayer. In an article written on the influence of Merton and Main, author Gregory Ryan says:

> It should be noted from the outset that neither Thomas Merton nor John Main lived at the theoretical level. Each one lived from the depths of his own heart and it is precisely this characteristic which presents a model for all women and men of our time. It is for this reason that Merton's influence and popularity continues to rise. It is for this reason that John Main's teaching on meditation has spread around the world.

Both monks would agree that the sickness which afflicts our world today is a morally bankrupt materialism gone mad, a kind of societal "heart disease." They would agree too, that the cure is to be found through a rediscovery of what it is that makes us human. The prescription for this recovery is silent prayer.[124]

On leaving Gethsemani, John Main told the monks, "I shall always remember with great affection these days among you." He had learned that his teaching on the way of prayer must be pursued more urgently than ever. He had also learned beyond any doubt that this was the work for the kingdom to which he was called to give the rest of his life.

Merton and Main: spiritual giants of the 20th century

How close were Thomas Merton and John Main in their spiritual pilgrimage? It would seem they were very close. These are the remarkable words of Merton in Calcutta a few days before his death: "The deepest level of communication is not communication but communion. It is wordless. It is beyond words and it is beyond concepts." That's a wonderful definition of John Main's teaching on meditation.

While Merton and Main were close in their thinking on prayer, there were differences in their emphasis and approach.

Neil McKenty, in *In the Stillness Dancing*, comments that Merton wrote a great deal *about* prayer; he wrote rather little about how he prayed. On the other hand, John Main was writing constantly about his own way of prayer. Merton was more of a writer; Main, more of a teacher. Main's writings, which almost exclusively stress Christian Meditation, seemed to transcend his personality, and John Main left a formal teaching about *how* to pray. Thomas Merton did not.

Meditation: a call to everyone

It is a credit to the genius of John Main that he synthesized the prayer teaching of John Cassian and the desert fathers, *The Cloud of Unknowing*, the spiritual teachings of Asia, and left a formal teaching on prayer for those of us in the 20th and 21st century. John Main was also unique in emphasizing that meditation or contemplation was a call to everyone. Even Thomas Merton once felt that the practice of contemplation was the spiritual prerogative of professed religious in contemplative orders like the Cistercians. He later changed his views, however. A few years before he died Merton had turned 180 degrees on this issue. "Who can desire the gift of contemplation?" he asked. "Everyone."

Merton and the Jesus mantra

It is very interesting that 11 years before his death in 1968, Merton indicated in a letter to a friend that he had come to use a mantra, the Jesus Prayer of the Eastern Christian tradition. (See Question 33 on the Jesus Prayer.) So in the final analysis, both Main and Merton had come to the spiritual insight that the practice of the mantra was the primary way to arrive at stillness and contemplative silence.

Merton's quotes on contemplative prayer

Contemplative prayer for Merton was finding one's true identity, one's true self. He often emphasized in his writing that meditation roots us in reality, leads us to an "awakened heart" and is really all about St. Paul's cry: "We do not know how to pray, but the Spirit prays within us" (Romans 8:26). Here are some additional thoughts by Merton on prayer:

- Sometimes meditation is nothing but an unsuccessful struggle to turn ourselves to God, to seek his face by faith. Any number of things beyond our control may make it impossible for one to meditate effectively. In that case faith and good will is sufficient. If one has made a really sincere and honest effort to turn oneself to God and cannot seem to get one's wits together at all, then the attempt will count as a meditation. This means that God, in His mercy, accepts our unsuccessful efforts.... Sometimes it happens that this interior helplessness is a sign of real progress in the interior life, for it makes us depend more completely and peacefully on the mercy of God.[125]

The seeds of contemplation are planted in every Christian soul

• The seeds of contemplation are planted in every Christian soul at baptism. But seeds must grow and develop before you reap the harvest. There are thousands of Christians walking about the face of the earth bearing in their bodies the infinite God of whom they know practically nothing. The seeds of contemplation have been planted in these souls, but they merely lie dormant. They do not germinate.[126]

• May my bones burn and ravens eat my flesh if I forget thee, contemplation.[127]

"Mary slept in the infinite tranquillity of God"

• And far beneath the movement of this silent cataclysm Mary slept in the infinite tranquillity of God, and God was a child curled up who slept in her and her veins were flooded with His wisdom which is night, which is starlight, which is silence. And her whole being was embraced in Him whom she embraced and they became tremendous *silence*.[128]

"If you have never had distractions you don't know how to pray"

• If you have never had any distractions you don't know how to pray...that is why it is useless to get upset when you cannot shake off distractions. In the first place you must realize that they are often unavoidable in the life of prayer. The necessity of...suffering submersion under a tidal wave of wild and inane images is one of the standard trials of the contemplative life.... If you are wise you will not pay any attention to these things: remain in simple attention to God.[129]

- For contemplation is always beyond our own knowledge, beyond our own light, beyond systems, beyond explanations, beyond discourse, beyond dialogue, beyond our own self.[130]

We will never be anything else but beginners

- In the spiritual life there are no tricks and no short cuts.... One cannot begin to face the real difficulties in the life of prayer and meditation unless one is first perfectly content to be a beginner and really experience oneself as one who knows little or nothing, and has a desperate need to learn the bare rudiments. Those who think they "know" from the beginning never, in fact, come to know anything.... We do not want to be beginners. But let us be convinced of the fact that we will never be anything else but beginners, all our life.[131]

QUESTION 42

Q. Could you give a brief account of the life of John Main?

A. The life of John Main spanned only 56 years (1926–1982), but in that short time he was a journalist, soldier, lawyer, diplomat, university lecturer, Benedictine monk and finally one of the great contemporary teachers of contemplative prayer.

His work took him from London to Ballinskelligs, Ireland, to Dublin, then Rome, Malaysia, back to Dublin, Rome, Washington, D.C., back to London and finally to Montreal, Canada. But John Main's greatest journey was a journey within, towards his own centre. He understood the words of Jesus: "The kingdom of God does not come in such a way as to be seen. No one will say 'look, here it is' or 'there it is,' because the kingdom of God is within you" (Luke 17:20-21).

This became John Main's final journey, leading thousands of people around the world to the discovery of this "kingdom within" through the daily, disciplined practice of Christian Meditation and the path of contemplative prayer.

John Main's parents

Douglas Victor (John) Main was born in London, England, on January 21, 1926, the fourth child of David and Eileen Main. (John was the religious name he assumed with the Benedictines many years later.) The other children included Kitty (born in 1920), Ian (1922), Yvonne (1924), Diane (1928) and Alan Patrick (1929).

John's father, David Main, was born in 1893 in Ballinskelligs, County Kerry, Ireland, in the family-owned hotel now known as the "Ballinskelligs Inn." David's father had come from Falkirk, Scotland, as superintendent of the newly established transatlantic cable station from Ireland to the United States. He and his wife founded the hotel that is still owned and run by the Main family in Ballinskelligs.

Eileen (Hurley) Main was born in County Meath, Ireland, in 1887. She received her early education in Belgium and became a nurse. In the great influenza epidemic of 1919, Eileen, at the age of 32, met David in Ballinskelligs, and they were married in Cork on February 7, 1920. After the birth of their first daughter, Kitty, David Main was transferred by Western Union from Ballinskelligs to London.

Early family life

John Main once said, "We were very happy in our home life and as well as being brothers and sisters, we were all great friends." In fact, it was in the heart of the family that

John Main first experienced the warmth of human love, a love that would give him such psychological stability in his later life. Sunday night was always family night in the Main family, for neighbours as well as friends, and usually included singing and games. In one game the participants wrote down the subject for a one-minute speech. Ian, the second-eldest child, was once outraged when he drew a subject suggested by his brother Douglas: "Early Byzantine Architecture."[132]

This kind of humour was a key element in the Main family life. In the book *John Main by Those Who Knew Him*,[133] Yvonne, one of his older sisters, recounts that "a few times as young children Douglas would celebrate mass with an altar on top of a chest of drawers. I was encouraged to be an altar girl but was frequently dismissed because I either started to laugh or rang the bell at the wrong time."

The Main home was one of deep Catholic faith and was grounded in St. Paul's injunction to honour the spirit rather than the letter of the law. If good food was going to spoil, Eileen Main would have no hesitation in overlooking the rule of Friday abstinence from meat. St. Benedict's injunction in his rule to "receive any guest as Christ" was enthusiastically followed in the Main family. Unwed mothers, alcoholics, abandoned wives, waifs and strays were welcomed into their home on numerous occasions.

"Ballinskelligs was always with him"

In 1932, at the age of six, John was not in robust health. He suffered from ear infections and his parents felt he should be sent to Ballinskelligs, County Kerry, Ireland, to build up his health through better food and air. He stayed there for part of the year, attended school and lived with his father's older brother, William and his wife Nell in the family hotel. "The influence of Ballinskelligs was always with him," a friend later said and, in fact, John Main fell in love with this remote part of Ireland and always felt Ballinskelligs to be his ancestral home.

Ballinskelligs had a mysterious but hidden influence on John Main's future life. Close to Ballinskelligs is the famous island site of Skellig Michael, rising 700 feet, seven miles out in the Atlantic off the Ballinskelligs coast. Irish monks built a monastic settlement at the summit of Skellig Michael in the sixth century, and monastic life continued there between Viking raids for over 700 years.

Main's relatives recount stories of Douglas asking fishermen to take him out to nearby islands, so it is possible he hitched a ride at this time with a fishing trawler to Skellig Michael. We do know that later in life he visited the Skellig and its monastic ruins with fellow students from Trinity College, Dublin. He was also deeply moved by the opening scene in the television program *Civilization*, where Sir Kenneth Clarke opens the series at the monastic enclosure on these Skellig rocks.

A deep conjecture about Skellig Michael

There is an even deeper question and more intriguing conjecture about Skellig Michael. Benedictine monk John Main is given the credit for rediscovering and recognizing the teaching of John Cassian (365–435) and the early Egyptian desert monks of repeating a short, sacred phrase in prayer to bring one to an interior silence in the presence of God. Cassian called it a "formula." John Main called it a "mantra." (See Question 32 on John Cassian.)

The mantra from Egypt to Gaul to Skellig Michael

John Cassian spent the last years of his life in Provence and brought the spirituality of the early Christian monks of the Egyptian desert to Gaul, with the aim of reforming Gallic monasticism. It was by way of Gaul that monasticism spread to settlements such as Skellig Michael off the west coast of Ireland. Cassian's teaching on prayer was popular in the early Celtic church. In later centuries it would be Celtic monks who would bring Christianity back to Europe.

It is interesting to note that the teaching of the mantra came from Egypt via Gaul to Ireland's Skellig Michael and that John Main, who spent part of his youth in sight of Skellig Michael, rediscovered this ancient prayer. What we can also surmise is that this direct contact with ancient Celtic monasticism was the impetus for his own eventual attraction to the Benedictine monastic life.

The war years

In 1937, at 11 years of age, John Main entered London's prestigious Westminster Cathedral Choir School. In 1939, at the beginning of World War II, he and his brother Ian were evacuated to a Jesuit school north of London. In 1942, when he was 17, he became a student journalist at a suburban London newspaper; the following year he enlisted in the Royal Corps of Signals and saw service in Belgium and Germany. Following the war he spent a few years with a religious congregation, the Canons Regular, followed by a law degree at Trinity College, Dublin.

In the direction of the East

John Main's next adventure in the direction of the East had friends bemused by his career choice. However, this was a pivotal decision, and its consequence was to change John Main's life as well as the lives of thousands of people around the world forever. In the spring of 1954 he applied to join the British Colonial Service. He was appointed to serve in Malaya (Malaysia); his first assignment was to study Chinese in London at the School of Oriental and African Studies. In one of his books he recalled the school's motto: "Knowledge is power."[154] John Main came to reject that motto. Years later he wrote, "The only real power is love."

In 1955, after taking up duties in Kuala Lumpur, he continued with his study of Chinese. One day John Main was sent on an apparently routine assignment to deliver a goodwill message from the Governor to Swami Satyananda, a Hindu monk who, as a child, was educated in a Catholic Mission and was founder of an orphanage school and ashram in Kuala Lumpur.

The day that changed his life

John Main thought he would quickly dispatch this rather routine assignment and be free for the rest of the day. But this visit changed his life and set in motion a gradual understanding of his true vocation. His goodwill mission accomplished, John Main asked the swami to discuss the spiritual base of the many good works carried out at the orphanage and school. The swami replied that the spiritual base of the ashram was the daily practice of meditation.

John Main realized that he was in the presence of a holy man, a teacher, a man of the spirit, whose faith was alive in love and service to others. Here is what John Main subsequently wrote many years later: "I was deeply impressed by his peacefulness and calm wisdom. For the Swami, the aim of meditation was the coming to awareness of the spirit who dwells in our hearts...who enfolds the whole universe, and in silence is loving to all."[135]

You must repeat this word faithfully, lovingly and continually

John Main was so moved by this passage from the ancient Indian scriptures, the Upanishads, and the swami's spiritual intensity that he asked to learn how to meditate. The swami agreed and invited him to come to visit him once a week. On his first visit the swami spoke about how to meditate:

> To meditate you must become silent. You must be still. And you must concentrate. In our tradition we know one way in which you can arrive at that stillness, that concentration. We use a word that we call a mantra. To meditate, what you must do is to

choose this word and then repeat it, faithfully, lovingly and continually. That is all there is to meditation. I really have nothing else to tell you. And now we will meditate.[136]

For 18 months John Main meditated with the swami; this encounter led Father John to join the pilgrimage of meditation and eventually to discover the Christian tradition of the mantra in the practice of the early desert fathers.

Becoming a Benedictine

In the summer of 1956, John Main returned to Dublin and obtained a post teaching administrative, Roman and international Law at Trinity College. Then, in 1959, at age 33, he entered the Benedictine Abbey of Ealing in London. After his novitiate, in 1962 he was sent to Rome to study theology at the International Benedictine College of San Anselmo. From there he visited monasteries in Italy, France and Germany, took hiking trips, spent summer holidays with his family in Ireland and was swept up in the exhilarating opening of the Second Vatican Council.

Discovering John Cassian

Eleven years later, John Main accepted an invitation to become headmaster at St. Anselm's Abbey School in Washington, D.C. While at St. Anselm's, he suggested one day to a young man that he read the book *Holy Wisdom* by a 17th-century Benedictine contemplative, Augustine Baker. The young man's response was so unexpectedly enthusiastic that John Main was moved to reread this spiritual classic. In this book he discovered the writings of the fourth-century desert monk John Cassian.

In the writings of Cassian, John Main found the link he had felt he was missing. What Cassian had learned in the deserts of Egypt was what John Main had learned from a Hindu monk three years before becoming a Benedictine monk. What they had in common was the teaching of the repetition of a word or short verse to bring one to an interior silence in prayer.

The first Christian Meditation Centre

In 1974, John Main started his first Christian Meditation group at the Ealing Abbey Prayer Centre in London. Then, in 1977, at the invitation of Bishop Leonard Crowley of Montreal, John Main founded a Benedictine Monastery there. It was dedicated to teaching and passing on this tradition of Christian Meditation to others. This work has now become a "monastery without walls" and is carried on around the world by the World Community of Christian Meditation based in London, England. (See Question 56 on the role of the World Community for Christian Meditation.)

The work is finished

John Main had always felt he would not live to an old age. He died of cancer on the morning of December 30, 1982, radiating a sense of presence and peace and surrounded by his Benedictine monastic community and Montreal meditators. But his work was done. He had left a full teaching on meditation for future generations.

Since his death, John Main's teaching on Christian Meditation has spread from the Benedictine Monastery he founded in Montreal to 60 countries around the world. Regarded as one of the 20th century's most important spiritual guides, John Main, through his teaching on this path of contemplative prayer, has transformed thousands of lives, and his influence continues to grow.[137]

QUESTION 43

Q. I read that the Benedictine monk Bede Griffiths once said, "In my experience, John Main is the best spiritual guide in the church today." Can you tell me more about Father Bede and his teaching on prayer?

A. Bede Griffiths was born December 17, 1906, into an English middle-class family of Anglican background. He was educated at Christ's Hospital School and later at Magdalen College, Oxford, where he studied English and philosophy. While at Oxford he rebelled against an education system which, in his opinion, served to over-emphasize the academic at the expense of the imaginative and intuitive. At Oxford, though, he became a lifelong friend and confidant of his tutor C.S. Lewis.

The golden string

In his autobiography, *The Golden String*,[138] Griffiths describes his attempt to live a life of radical simplicity, close to nature, with two companions in a Cotswold cottage after they left Oxford in 1929. Griffiths leaned towards agnosticism and none of the three were practising Christians. Following the Cotswold experiment in community living, a personal crisis led to a spiritual experience of God, to becoming a Catholic and, in 1933, entering Prinknish Benedictine Abbey. He was ordained a priest in 1940 and remained at Prinknish until 1953.

"To find the other half of my soul"

At Prinknish, a visiting Indian priest one day asked whether anyone would be willing to come to India and help found a religious community. Griffiths was eager to go. He had not only studied Indian and Chinese scripture but had an interest in Eastern religions and spirituality which had been kindled in him by a Jewish woman, Toni Sussmann, who had taught him yoga. (Sussmann directed a yoga and meditation centre in London.) On departing for

India in 1955, Griffiths predicted that he was leaving "to find the other half of my soul."

In 1958 he joined the Cistercian Abbey of Kurisumala, India, and in 1968 he took leadership of the ashram of Saccidananda (hermitage of the Holy Trinity) or, as it is more commonly called today, Shantivanum ("Forest of Peace"), in Tamil Nadu, southern India. It was here that Bede Griffiths sought to "inculturate" Christianity and Benedictine monastic life into an Indian context by adopting the simple lifestyle (in food and dress) of India's rural population.

He dressed as a *sannyasa* with his *kavi* (orange robe) and walked barefoot. He felt that an ashram should emphasize the practice of meditation and contemplative prayer and also be open to all religions. As a pioneer in interreligious dialogue he opened Shantivanum to interfaith meetings and was a keynote speaker at such meetings around the world. The ashram eventually drew thousands of visitors each year, including meditators and many young people, especially from Western countries. They found Bede open and humble, with a warm and radiant heart and a disarming innocence.

Father Bede on meditation

In his prayer life Father Bede practised meditation using the mantra of the Jesus Prayer (see Question 33 on the Jesus Prayer). He wrote:

> Personally, I find that meditation, morning and evening, every day, is the best and most direct method of getting in touch with reality. In meditation, I try to let go of everything of the outer world of the senses, of the inner world of thoughts, and listen to the inner voice, the voice of the Word, which comes in the silence, in the stillness when all activity of body and mind cease. Then, in the silence, I become aware of the presence of God,

and I try to keep that awareness during the day. In a bus or a train or travelling by air, in work or study or talking and relating to others, I try to be aware of this presence in everyone and in everything. And the Jesus prayer is what keeps me aware of the presence.

So prayer for me is the practice of the presence of God in all situations, in the midst of noise and distractions of all sorts, of pain and suffering and death, as in times of peace and quiet, of joy and friendship, of prayer and silence, the presence is always there. For me, the Jesus prayer is just a way of keeping in the presence of God.[139]

His views on the feminine

An enduring legacy of Father Bede are his views on the feminine and his criticism of the overwhelming masculinity of Western Christianity. He sided with Julian of Norwich on the concept of God as mother and he believed the acceptance of this understanding of the feminine aspect of God would eventually lead to women gaining their rightful place in the church. (See Question 35 on Julian of Norwich.) He bemoaned the fact that "we have nothing but male images of God."

Early on the morning of January 25, 1990, as he was sitting on the veranda of his hut at Shantivanum meditating, he had a severe stroke. His life hung in the balance for a week as he lay motionless and speechless. After his recovery he regarded the stroke as a mystical experience, since the right side of the brain, which was not paralysed by the stroke, opened him up to a breakthrough to the feminine. He subsequently wrote, "I was very masculine and patriarchal and had been developing the left brain all this time. Now the right brain, the feminine came and hit me."

This profound inner experience took his spiritual or psyche energy from his head to his heart and he now saw love as the basic principle of the entire universe. He wrote, "I find myself in the void, but the void is totally saturated with love." He summed up this fusing of the masculine and feminine in saying, "God is not simply in the light, in the intelligible world, in the rational order. God is in the darkness, in the womb, in the mother.... the darkness is the womb of life." He had finally found the other half of his soul that he had hoped to find on coming to India.

To the "further shore" at 87

Father Bede passed to the "further shore" on May 13, 1993, at Shantivanum. He was 87. Father Laurence Freeman, who gave the homily at the "Mass in Thanksgiving for the Life and Teaching of Bede Griffiths" on June 15, 1993, in Westminster Cathedral, London, has summed up Bede's life very succinctly: "Through extensive travels in America, Europe and Australia in his later years, Father Bede developed the vision of modern life and religion which is his abiding legacy. He saw the modern world at a crossroads comparable to only two or three such epochs in human history. And he saw the recovery of a spiritual vision as an essential means for its survival."

The sometimes exclusive claims and dualistic thinking of the Semitic religions of Judaism, Christianity and Islam, which had been responsible for so many wars and so much hatred, needed, he believed, to be touched by the *advaita* or non-dualism and the contemplative priority of *experience* of the Asian religions. This idea was developed brilliantly in his 1982 book, *The Marriage of East and West*.[140]

The mantra as a bridge between East and West

As mentioned, the deepest source of Griffiths' vision was his own spiritual path of meditation. Since the 1940s he had practised the Jesus Prayer, a form of the interior and non-discursive prayer of the heart that he saw as an essential complement to all the forms of external worship.

In the teaching of the Christian tradition of meditation by his fellow Benedictine, John Main, he discovered meditation and the way of the mantra as an essential bridge between East and West.

At the John Main Seminar that he led at New Harmony, Indiana, in 1991, Griffiths used John Main's thought to crystallize his own vision of prayer and contemporary spiritual needs, particularly the need for community. These Seminar talks, published as *The New Creation in Christ*, describe Griffiths' profound sense of the crisis facing modern humanity, but also his sense of hope and faith.[141]

A religious prophet of modern times

Bede Griffiths is one of the great religious prophets of modern times. His influence will continue to be felt not only in those he has inspired but through the writings he left to be published after his death. He testifies to the possibility, rarely achieved in a skeptical age, of uniting intellect with spirit and of their integration in a human nature of great gentleness and profound compassion for others, through all the adventures of a long life of seeking and sharing God.[142]

QUESTION 44

Q. I am reading the author Carlo Carretto, who seems to echo Father John Main's teaching on silence in prayer. Could you comment on Carretto's life and teaching?

A. Carlo Carretto was born in 1910. From 1946 to 1952 he was president of Catholic Action in Italy. In 1954 he went into the Sahara Desert to join the Little Brothers of Jesus, inspired by the spirituality of Charles de Foucauld. For 24 years, until his death in 1988 at the age of 78, he wrote 15 books, which are estimated to have reached millions of readers worldwide, and he is regarded as one of the great spiritual writers of our time.

His early life

Born in 1910 in Northern Piedmont, Italy, Carlo was the third of six children, four of whom entered the religious life. One of his younger brothers became a bishop in Thailand. Educated at a Salesian Oratory, Carretto became a primary school teacher and went on to take a degree in history and philosophy. However, it was in Catholic Action – a lay movement of students and young people whose aim was to make the Gospel relevant to the working and student environment – that he found a new outlet for his creative energies. He always spoke with enthusiasm about the effect Catholic Action had on his life: "It took me by the hand and walked with me, it fed me with the word, it offered me friendship, it taught me how to fight, it helped me to know Christ, it inserted me alive into a living reality."

On seeking prayer and silence

The next step in his life is outlined by Robert Ellsberg in an introduction to the *Selected Writings of Carlo Carretto*.[143] Says Ellsberg: "On a deeper level he had become disillusioned with big movements, loud rallies and activism, even on behalf of the church, that were not sustained by an attitude of prayer and an openness to silence." (See Question 49 on prayer and action.)

After 20 years as a leader with Catholic Action, Carlo was now ready to serve God in a new way. His flight to the desert shocked his friends and fellow workers, but explained that he felt it was a call from God; "leave everything and come with me into the desert. It is not your acts and deeds that I want: I want your *prayer*, your *love*." His arrival in the Sahara in 1954 opened up a completely different life of daily menial labor, solitude and a time for prayer and silence. Soon after his arrival an improperly administered injection in one of his legs left him crippled for life. However, out of his desert experience came an understanding that in fact he still must seek God in his fellow human beings.

For the next 10 years Carretto lived as a desert hermit, but in 1972 his classic *Letters from the Desert* was published and clearly established him as one of the great spiritual voices of the 20th century.[144]

His writing was also responsible for popularizing the life of another desert monk, Charles de Foucauld. Foucauld spent 15 years in the desert, and was killed in 1916 by Tuareg rebels. In 1933, long after Foucauld's death, Rene Voillaime and four companions left France for the Sahara and founded the Little Brothers of Jesus. This was followed by the founding of the Little Sisters of Jesus; both fraternities have spread around the world. Robert Kiely, former Director of the Guiding Board, World Community for Christian Meditation, has written, "Carlo Carretto speaks to us from the desert, in a warm Italian voice filled with the hope, forgiveness and joy of the Gospels. To read his words is to share in the wisdom and peace of his life in Christ."

Back to the Umbrian Hills

In 1965 he joined an experiential community near Assisi in the Umbrian Hills in Italy, an offshoot of the Little Brothers, that sought spiritual renewal for the laity. It was here that he began to give retreats and seminars and wrote most of his books. He remained a lay brother all his life and constantly affirmed "the dignity of the laity."

In his later years he demonstrated a commitment to poverty and non-violence. He continued to be suspicious of large structures and institutions, yet he always exhibited a spirit of hope and love, a joyous spirituality, especially as he neared death.

Contemplative life in the midst of the world

In summing up his life Robert Ellsberg writes:

Carretto represented an ascetic, yet joy-filled spirituality available to lay people, even in the midst of pressing obligations, even amidst the din of city noise, even in the midst of poverty and suffering. He showed that a life of prayer need not, indeed must not, relieve us of a passion for social justice and a spirit of solidarity with the least of our brothers and sisters.

At the same time he reminded social activists that in the midst of their good works they must preserve a place of stillness, a place where they can listen to the word of God, and find renewal. Essentially Carretto showed that it was possible to live a contemplative life in the midst of the world – the desert, after all, is really everywhere. The heart of the Gospel is to make of ourselves an oasis of love in whatever desert we might find ourselves. That was the challenge of his life.[145]

Quotations from Carlo Carretto

A recurring theme in Carlo Carretto's books is his dying to the world of power, of politics, and his pilgrimage to the emptiness of the desert, the desert of the Spirit. There is a saying that he burnt his address book and went into the desert to learn to pray. Here are some of his key quotations about the desert and prayer, selected from among his many books:

- I've done a lot of work for the church, I'm aware of it. It has been my only thought, my only care. I have raced hard and covered as many miles as the most committed missionary. At a certain point it occurred to me that what the church lacked was not work, activity, the building of projects or a commitment to bring in souls. What was missing, *or at least was scarce, was the element of prayer, meditation, self-giving, intimacy with God, fidelity to the Holy Spirit and the conviction that He was the real builder of the church*: in a word the supernatural element. Let me make myself clear: people of action are needed in the church but we have to be very careful that their *action does not smother the more delicate but much more important element of prayer.*[146]

Only with the deepest silence can we hear God's call

- God's call is mysterious; it comes in the darkness of faith. It is so fine, so subtle, that it is only with the deepest silence within us that we can hear it.[147]

- "Come into the desert." There is something much greater than human action: prayer; and it has a power much stronger than human words.[148]

- The closer you come to God as you ascend the slopes of contemplation, the greater grows your craving to love human beings on the level of action.[149]

"The body, too, has its part to play in prayer"

- With a little imagination, even a hole under the stairs, even a garret, can become our *poustinia*, our desert where we can recollect ourselves and savour silence and prayer…. The body too has its part to play in prayer…the external posture sometimes becomes a testimony to our faith.[150]

"To be children in God's arms, silent, loving, rejoicing"

- This is the highest state of prayer: to be children in God's arms, silent, loving, rejoicing…choose one little word or a little phrase which well expresses your love for him; and then go on repeating it in peace, without trying to form thoughts, motionless in love before God who is love. And with this word or this phrase, transformed into an arrow of steel, a symbol of your love, beat again and again against God's thick cloud of unknowing.[151]

QUESTION 45

Q. I have seen a photo of Father Laurence Freeman speaking to over a hundred of Mother Teresa's novices in Calcutta. Was Mother Teresa supportive of Christian Meditation/contemplative prayer? Did she write on this subject?

A. Father Laurence and meditators from other parts of the world visited Mother Teresa on numerous occasions before her death. I had the opportunity of visiting and talking to Mother Teresa in January 1991 in Bombay and Calcutta and can attest to her great commitment to contemplative spirituality.

As foundress of the Missionaries of Charity, Mother Teresa had a lifetime commitment to silence and stillness in prayer combined with extraordinary service and compassion to the most needy of this world. She had a deep understanding of the relationship between contemplative prayer and action and ensured that twice-daily times of silent prayer were an integral part of the morning and evening schedule of her sisters.

Mother Teresa and contemplative prayer

Meditators are aware that the flame of love that springs from prayer can suddenly burst forth. Like the prophets of old, the person who meditates often has an inner eye awakened to suffering and injustice in the world. We see this in Mother Teresa, who was involved in the suffering and anguish of the world around her and yet was deeply committed to the power source, the presence of Christ she found in the silence of prayer. Here are a few of her thoughts on the importance of this prayerful silence and the relationship between prayer and action:

"We need silence to be able to touch souls"

- We need to find God, and He cannot be found in noise and restlessness. See how nature, the trees, the flowers, and the grass grow in perfect silence. See the stars, the moon, and the sun, how they move in silence. The Apostle said, "We will give ourselves continually at prayer and to the ministry of the Word." For the more we receive in silent prayer, the more we can give in our active life. We need silence to be able to touch souls. The essential thing is not what we say, but what God says to us.[152]

· We [Missionaries of Charity] are called to be contemplatives in the world.[153]

"God is the friend of silence"

· God is the friend of silence. His language is silence. Be still and know that I am God. He requires us to be silent to discover Him. In the silence of the heart, He speaks to us.

Jesus spent forty days before beginning his public life in silence. He often retired alone, spent the night on the mountain in silence and prayer. He who spoke with authority spent his early life in silence.

We need silence to be alone with God...to listen to him, to ponder his words deep in our hearts. We need to be alone with God in silence to be renewed and to be transformed. Silence gives us a new outlook on life. In it we are filled with the energy of God Himself, which makes us do all things with joy.[154]

"Prayer is oneness with Christ"

· In reality, there is only one prayer, only one substantial prayer: Christ himself. There is only one voice which rises above the face of the earth: the voice of Christ. Prayer is oneness with Christ.

When times come when we can't pray, it is very simple: if Jesus is in my heart, let Him pray, let Him talk to His Father in the silence of my heart.

Since I cannot speak, He will speak; since I cannot pray, He will pray.[155]

"Contemplatives in the heart of the world"

- Prayer is nothing but that complete surrender, complete oneness with Christ. And this is what makes us contemplatives in the heart of the world; for we are twenty-four hours then in His presence: in the hungry, in the naked, in the homeless, in the unwanted, unloved, uncared for. For Jesus said, "Whatever you do to the least of my brethren, you do it to me."[156]

"Jesus is always waiting for us in silence"

- Jesus is always waiting for us in silence. In this silence He listens to us; it is there that He speaks to our souls. And there, we hear His voice. Interior silence is very difficult, but we must make the effort to pray. In this silence we find a new energy and a real unity. God's energy becomes ours, allowing us to perform things well.[157]

- A soul of prayer can make progress without recourse to words, by learning to listen, to be present to Christ, and to look toward Him.[158]

"If you want to learn to pray, keep silence"

- If we neglect prayer and if the branch is not connected with the vine, it will die. That connecting of the branch to the vine is prayer. If that connection is there then love is there, then joy is there, and we will be the sunshine of God's love, the hope of eternal happiness, the flame of burning love. Why? Because we are one with Jesus. If you sincerely want to learn to pray: keep silence.[159]

- You should spend at least half an hour in the morning, and an hour at night in prayer. You can pray while you work. Work doesn't stop prayer, and prayer doesn't stop work.[160]

"My secret is quite simple. I pray."

- Interviewer: "Mother Teresa, you love people whom others regard as human debris. What is your secret?"

  Mother Teresa: "My secret is quite simple. I pray."[161]

- Let us adore Jesus in our hearts, who spent thirty years out of thirty-three in silence; who began his public life by spending forty days in silence; who often retired alone to spend the night on a mountain in silence.[162]

QUESTION 46

Q. I attended the John Main Seminar in England in 1992, which featured Jean Vanier, founder of the L'Arche Community for people who are mentally challenged. Can you bring me up to date on the life of Jean Vanier and his views on the Christian Meditation tradition of prayer?

A. Having attended that 1992 seminar myself, I was deeply and profoundly moved not only by Vanier's great love and compassion for the vulnerability and weakness of people with developmental disabilities but also by his conviction that this love and compassion offered at L'Arche must flow increasingly from prayer. Jean also offered his advice and expertise on the development of the constitution of the World Community for Christian Meditation.

The great awakening

In August 1964, when Jean Vanier was 34 years of age and a philosophy teacher at the University of Toronto, he visited a Dominican priest, Father Thomas Philippe, in the small French village of Trosly-Breuil. Father Thomas, a chaplain at an institution for 30 men with mental disabilities, invited Jean to meet some of the men. This experience was to change Jean's life forever. He was deeply moved by the vulnerability of the men and wrote, "Up to that time I knew only about Aristotle and warships." (He

had been an officer in the Canadian and British navies.)
He continues:

> I saw in the faces of these men anger and violence
> and tenderness. Here was something terrifying and
> yet profoundly of God. I sensed in all their flesh
> and their being a primal cry. "Do you love me?"

Jean Vanier writes that he bought a cottage in Trosly-
Breuil and invited two mentally disabled men, Raphael
Simi and Philippe Seux, to join him in a community of
three. He says:

> I had no idea where it would lead but I knew that
> Jesus wanted me to do this and that I had taken an
> irreversible step; and while I had taken this step
> out of a desire to serve the poor, I gradually
> learned that Raphael and Philippe were indeed
> helping me to discover my own poverty.[163]

God chooses the weak to confound the strong

Later Vanier came to understand that God's special presence in the weak and outcast echoed St. Paul's teaching
that God has "chosen the weak to confound the strong" (I
Corinthians 1:27). Jean Vanier came to a strong belief that
God reveals his presence in *weakness* and *littleness.* In one
of his talks he muses on the *littleness* of the Resurrection:
"Christ did not appear on the rooftops saying, 'I'm back,
I've won.' He appeared quietly as a workman in a cemetery."

From the small house at Trosly-Breuil, Vanier started
L'Arche (the ark), named after Noah's ark in the Bible. The
L'Arche Community has now mushroomed to over 100
houses in 29 countries around the world. Jean has given
over the active leadership to others, but as an elder states-
man continues to guide the Community and travels the
world visiting L'Arche houses and giving retreats and
seminars.[164]

The Vanier family and meditation

Jean Vanier and his family have had a long commitment to the path of Christian meditation. In the biography of Jean's mother, entitled *One Woman's Journey: A Portrait of Pauline Vanier*,[165] authors Deborah Cowley and George Cowley describe the weekly Christian meditation group led by Pauline Vanier at the L'Arche Community in France. Pauline Vanier played John Main tapes and attracted L'Arche assistants from around the world to her weekly group meetings.

As mentioned, the activity in L'Arche communities flows increasingly from prayer. Jean Vanier has indicated he would be happy to see Christian Meditation groups started in L'Arche houses. Two such communities in Kerala, India, and Edmonton, Canada, subsequently started Christian Meditation groups.

Jean Vanier on contemplative prayer

Like Mother Teresa, Jean Vanier recognizes that faith and prayer lie at the core of all his work. He speaks of prayer as his "oxygen"; like Mother Teresa, he sees prayer as the religious base for his work and the work of L'Arche. Here are a few thoughts by Jean Vanier on the importance of silence in prayer.

- Prayer is to be in contact with our own Centre. It is to let Jesus make his home in us and to make our home in him.

- A spiritual life...is especially necessary for the weak...the mentally handicapped...in love, fraternity, prayer and silence. Their religious life will not primarily be one of action but rather that of contemplation, that is the life of one ...who receives peace and radiates it and who lives a life nourished by prayer.

- When we live in community and everyday life is busy and difficult, it is absolutely essential for us to have moments alone to pray and meet God in silence and quietness.

- Prayer is like a secret garden made up of silence and rest and inwardness.

- For prayer is the opening of our being to the call of love, letting ourselves be opened to peace, to open ourselves to the reality of the word and of our Father, to enter into silence, to become conscious of love, to retreat from over activity, to rest and have periods of quiet.

- We all agree that to be still is important from all points of view, humanly, spiritually, psychologically, for it brings equilibrium, peace and can, in fact, increase our ability to be active.[166]

PART FOUR

Some Questions About the Journey of Contemplative Prayer

QUESTION 47

Q. What is the role of Mary on the contemplative journey?

A. John Main felt so strongly about Mary's role in our spiritual journey that he wrote a beautiful treatise entitled *The Other-Centredness of Mary*. It is contained in the book *Community of Love*.[167] In this treatise John Main points out that Mary is really the model and mother of the contemplative life for Christians because she is essentially described in the gospel as a person of prayer. He goes on to say that the secret of Mary's universal appeal in our day is her interiority and her other-centredness. In expanding this understanding of Mary, John Main says:

> The essential Christian insight which Mary exemplifies in Luke's Gospel is poverty of spirit. This is purity of heart because it is unsullied by the intrusion of the egotistic will seeking for experience, desiring holiness, objectifying the Spirit or creating God in its own image. Mary reveals the basic simplicity of the Christian response in a poverty of spirit that consists in turning wholly to God, wholly away from self.[168]

This poverty of spirit and turning away from self is, of course, the heart of our Christian Meditation practice. Like Mary, we must continually seek to project our consciousness away from self. John Main points out that her other-centredness makes Mary our model as meditators.

Mary and the prayer of the heart

Christian Meditation is often referred to as "the prayer of the heart" (see Question 26 on the prayer of the heart). Mary's entire life was lived in her heart. St. Luke mentions Mary's heart twice in his gospel. At the nativity Mary reflects on the words of the shepherds: "As for Mary, she treasured these things and pondered them in her heart" (Luke 2:19). At the finding of the child Jesus in the temple, "His mother stored up all these things in her heart" (Luke

2:51). Mary knew the power of the Spirit at work in her heart. It is little wonder that her life was one of contemplation.

Father Patrick Eastman, editor of the spiritual journal *Monos*, comments that in her surrender at the Annunciation,

> Mary is still and silent, she hears the spoken word and gives consent for that spoken word to be enfleshed within her and God breathes upon her and it is done. The word is made flesh and comes to bring healing into a broken world and the Church as Body of Christ is born. Now let us move to our times of prayer. Is not the same process at work? We are invited by God's grace to be still and silent that we may hear the word spoken to us. Prayer then becomes a silence and stillness where we surrender to God.[169]

Mary's role is to give birth to Jesus in our hearts

Mary is often termed the "listening heart of Israel" and "the woman wrapped in silence." But to listen does require silence. In her listening, Mary's silence was one of deep joy as she rejoiced in God her saviour (Luke 1:47).

In our final view of Mary in the Acts of the Apostles, we see her still at prayer with the apostles in the upper room in Jerusalem, waiting for the coming of the Spirit (1:14). Perhaps that is ultimately her role with those who meditate: to bring that Spirit to us in the silence; to give birth to Jesus in our hearts. Our role in meditation is to wait in silence and faith for the utterance of his word within us.

Mary's famous fiat, "Let it be done unto me according to your word" (Luke 1:38) is the same fiat we must express on the path of Christian Meditation. In meditation we must be open to whatever happens, whether it is the sense of God's presence or absence, distractions or silence; everything must be totally accepted in the spirit of Mary's fiat.

Mary: flooded with contemplative love

Mary spoke few words in her humble, hidden life. Flooded with contemplative love, she enjoyed being for the most part silent before the Lord. In that respect she becomes the fully conscious, integrated human being worthy of imitation by all meditators.

QUESTION 48

Q. What is the desert experience or the "dark night of the soul" as it relates to meditation?

A. As we start off on the journey of meditation we often experience peace, calm, joy, sweetness and what are termed *consolations.* Unfortunately, many of us become attached to these gifts and fail to see that a predictable part of each person's spiritual journey will be the "desert experience."

In our spiritual journey this can be a period of aridity, of turbulence, of distractions, of nothingness where God seems to have disappeared. We cannot find him. He seems to have left us. This stage of the journey is our time in the desert or wilderness.

St. John of the Cross calls it the "dark night of the soul." He says it is a time where there is no consolation of any kind, where we feel deserted by God. He terms it a sensory dark night of purgation. In the *Dark Night* he writes: "When God sees that they [souls] have grown a little, he weans them from the sweet breast so that they might be strengthened, lays aside their swaddling bands, and puts them down from his arms that they may grow accustomed to walking by themselves."[170]

God is in the desert; don't be afraid to enter there

Both the Old and New Testaments and many contemporary writers on spirituality speak of the importance of the desert experience on one's spiritual journey. They all point to the desert as a time of "waiting upon God," but also as a time of purification, loneliness, isolation, dryness, anguish and yet, paradoxically, a time of inner joy. The desert seems to be a necessary condition of the soul prior to union with God.

There are four short quotations that are pertinent to the desert. The first is from the New Testament. Referring to Jesus, Luke says, "But he himself retired to the desert and prayed there." (5:16) The second is from Hosea, in the Old Testament: God says, "I will lead you to the desert and speak to your heart." (2:16). The third quotation is from Thomas Merton, who said, "Contemplative prayer is simply the preference for the desert, for emptiness, for poverty." The final quotation is by Father Robert Wild, who has written in *The Post-Charismatic Experience*: "God is in the desert. Don't be afraid to enter there. He really cannot be found anywhere else.... He loves you and awaits in the desert to embrace you and lead you home."[171]

God seems a billion light years away

The desert experience is generally a time of cleansing and pruning. The desert experience means an emptying of our self-centredness. For those on the path of meditation the desert experience often means aridity and dryness, boredom, and even the sense of being abandoned by God. We are no longer aware of God's loving presence in our daily times of meditation.

It can especially be a time of endless distractions in meditation when interior silence seems very far away. One contemporary meditator has put the desert experience in modern terms: "God seems a billion light years away. He has simply disappeared. He is inexplicably absent." There is certainly an absence of consolations in the desert.

In talking about the desert, Thomas Merton says:

The prospect of this wilderness is something that so appals most people that they refuse to enter upon its burning sands and travel amongst its rocks. They cannot believe that contemplation and sanctity are to be found in a desolation where there is no food and no shelter and no refreshment for their imagination and intellect and the desires of their nature.[172]

In our personal lives, the desert experience can be a time of trauma, loss of a loved one, sickness, emotional or physical suffering, loneliness, separation, divorce, difficulties in our work situation, or the physical problems of old age. Personal difficulties can lead us into the desert.

The desert: a time of spiritual testing

As Jesus was tempted in the desert, so we too will be tempted. Again the desert is a place of spiritual testing. In the desert of emptiness and dryness where we feel that God is absent, we can be tempted to skip our meditation periods. We can rationalize that we will make it up later, that we are not in the right mood for meditation, or that we need to devote ourselves to some apostolic action or good works. Behind our rationalization lies a feeling of resentment. We are hurt. God seems to have let us down. We say to ourselves, "If I am generous enough to give God two half-hours of my time in meditation each day, God could at least give me a little encouragement." This is the self-analysis and self-questioning of our meditation that John Main begs us to avoid. This is the self-concern we are meant to leave behind in meditation.

Becoming a desert traveller

What is happening in the desert experience is echoed in St. Paul's words to the Corinthians: "I fed you with milk, and did not give you solid food because you were not ready for it" (1 Corinthians 3:2). In the desert the Lord is giving us more substantial food and weaning us from the milk of our earlier days on the path of meditation. This is the time he teaches us to detach ourselves from consolations and spiritual delights and to become a desert traveller. We must learn to live in the desert, where the path often seems obscure and God seems to have disappeared. The desert requires faith when we appear to be lost and when fear enters the recesses of our hearts. The secret of surviving and even flourishing in the desert is a loving trust and faith in the Lord. As meditators in the desert experience we all discover a special intimacy and nearness to God.

God follows his own timetable in the desert experience

In our own desert experience and in the poverty and emptiness of meditation, we too have to learn to accept our state of helplessness so that God can fill us with himself. Thomas Merton puts this paradox so well. He says, "Only when we are able to *let go* of everything within us, all desire to see, to know, to taste and to experience the consolation of God, only then are we *truly* able to experience that presence" [author's italics]. Jesus says, "The one who will lose their life will save it" (Matthew 10:39).

In meditation the desert experience tells us that we have to trust that God is present and that he loves us even when he seems permanently absent. Until he comes to deliver us we have to go on persevering in our periods of meditation. God follows his own timetable in the desert experience.

Meditation and the desert experience

The desert experience challenges us to overcome our self-centredness. Can we meditate without concern for where God is leading us? Can we meditate faithfully when distractions bombard us? Can we meditate when nothing "happens" in meditation? Can we give up our desire to possess God and shed all desire for spiritual consolation in meditation? Can we meditate with ever-deepening generosity? If we can't, our faith will never be pure. And so the desert purifies our motives. The desert challenges us to forget about ourselves in prayer. The desert eats away at our self-centredness. Again, the desert is a place where we are tempted and tested, brought to self-knowledge, purified and strengthened through faith.[173]

God lives in the desert and leads us

But there is a great paradox about the desert experience. The desert can also be a place of beauty, of rest, of peace, a place where we can hear God in the silence of our own heart, where at times we can remotely sense his presence, where our eyes are beginning to open. With our fidelity to meditation we will come to love the desert.

God looked after the Israelites in the desert and fed them with food from heaven. The desert is not a place of sadness. It can be a place of great joy. There are flowers between the sand and rocks, there are living things, there is beauty. God lives in the desert and leads us on.

The desert experience may seem like it lasts for a long time, but salvation history assures us the desert does not last forever.

God guides us through the desert. He will never permit us to be tried beyond our strength, or to experience his absence beyond the limits of our endurance. It is by the power of God's grace and his Holy Spirit present in us that we can say "yes" to his apparent absence in our desert experience.

In the desert, life goes on

The paradox is this: our feelings of loneliness and inner emptiness in the desert can simultaneously coexist in our hearts along with deep peace, joy and even a sense of humour. In the desert we can have a compassionate love and a transforming hope and joy in the risen Christ dwelling within us. In the desert, life goes on.

The song of the desert should be "Alleluia!"

We must remember that the Promised Land that comes after the desert experience is brimming with delights and is the scriptural equivalent to union with God. God continually draws us through the desert of this life to himself. He stands at the far side of the desert waiting for us. Thomas Merton has written that the song of the desert should be "Alleluia!" The desert experience, which every journey of meditation will include, opens us to the joy of our emptiness in the face of God's infinite, loving goodness. The path that leads through the desert leads to peace, love and joy.

God waits at the far side of the desert

Here are Isaiah's inspiring and consoling words about life in the desert:

> Let the wilderness and the dry lands exult, let the wasteland rejoice and bloom, let it bring forth flowers...let it rejoice and sing for joy. Strengthen all weary hands, steady all trembling knees and say to all faint hearts, courage! Do not be afraid. Look, your God is coming; He is coming to save you. Water gushes in the desert, streams in the wasteland, the scorched earth becomes a lake, and the parched land springs of water. And through it will run a highway undefiled which shall be called the sacred way; the unclean may not travel by it, nor fools stray along it. They will come...shouting for joy, everlasting joy on their faces, joy and gladness will go with them and sorrow and lament be ended (Isaiah 35:6-10).

On the far side of the desert, waiting, is the Promised Land.

QUESTION 49

Q. When I began meditating I felt that meditation would lead me to self-fulfillment, inner healing, peace and tranquility. Now I seem to be getting a bigger picture, that meditation is leading me to become more involved with my family, my community and the world around me. Can you clarify this relationship between prayer and action?

A. I believe that one day Jesus gave us the perfect example of this balanced integration of prayer and action. This is beautifully described in the Gospel of Mark 1:35-38:

> In the morning, while it was still very dark, Jesus got up and went out to a deserted place, and there he prayed. And Simon and his companions hunted for him. When they found him, they said to him, "Everyone is searching for you."

> He answered, 'Let us go on to the neighbouring towns, so that I may proclaim the message there also; for that is what I came out to do.'

Mark points out that Jesus gets up early in the morning to pray and yet later is responsive to his disciples when they suggest there is some work to do that day in sharing the "good news." Here is that balanced relationship between prayer and action, a time for prayer and a time for action.

And again in the Gospel of Luke, "Now more than ever the word about Jesus spread abroad; many crowds would gather to hear and be cured of their diseases. But he would withdraw to deserted places and pray" (Luke 5:15-16).

Is meditation an escape from life?

Unfortunately, people feel that meditation is an escape from life and from the world of reality. A woman in the city where I live once said to a meditator, "I just don't trust that meditation business. All you meditators do is sit in a cave and contemplate your belly button while the rest of the world goes hungry." Most of us who meditate must, at one time or another, face people who may be suspicious of what is happening to us on the meditative journey. People often look to see if we are using prayer as an escape from our everyday lives and responsibilities.

John Main was adamant that meditation, far from being an escape from life, actually propels one into life and to love and compassion for others. Another teacher, Jesuit Father William Johnston, faces this problem head on when he says in his book *Silent Music*:

> In the final analysis meditation is a love affair. And love is the most powerful energy in the universe. The great irony of meditation is that we become more immersed in the here-and-now. When we are liberated from our false egos, we begin to know and love others at a deeper level of awareness. We reach out with a new found compassion to our family, friends, the less fortunate.[174]

The personal fruits of prayer that St. Paul talks about can also include a call to action. As Father Johnston points out, the flame of love that springs from prayer can suddenly burst forth. Like the prophets of old, the person who meditates often has an inner eye awakened to suffering and injustice in the world and suddenly discovers that he or she cannot refuse the call to action. The path of meditation often leads to a compassion for the poor, the sick, the oppressed, the weak, the underprivileged, the needy.

Mother Teresa and Jean Vanier

We see this in the lives of Mother Teresa and Jean Vanier (see Questions 45 and 46). Both chose to be involved in the conflicts, suffering and anguish of others, and yet both made the commitment to silence in prayer. Apart from these great spiritual witnesses, there are a host of meditators around the world who integrate their daily meditation with love, commitment and service to family and community. The late Father Henri Nouwen, who worked at one of Jean Vanier's houses in Ontario, Canada, said that contemplatives are not the ones who withdraw from the world to save their own soul, but rather the ones who enter into the centre of the world and pray there.

Prayer must lead us outward to others

Thomas Merton did not withdraw from the world in his Kentucky hermitage. (See Question 41 on Thomas Merton.) Merton became publicly involved in both the civil rights and peace movements and saw social concerns and justice issues as an integral part of his contemplative journey. Merton felt strongly that the unmasking of illusion belonged to the essence of the contemplative life, and that one must live out the life of contemplation among one's fellow human beings.

Merton is quoted in *Thomas Merton on Prayer* as saying, "All prayer must lead us outwards to others."[175] He emphasizes this when he says that if we experience God in silent prayer, we experience God not for ourselves alone but also for others. As Merton saw it, contemplation at its highest intensity becomes a reservoir of spiritual vitality that pours itself out in the most varied kinds of social involvement.

Meditation results in a wellspring of compassion

Buddhists also clearly see the connection between meditation and compassion for others. Joseph Goldstein, a Buddhist teacher of meditation, says in *Insight Meditation: The Practice of Freedom*: "Over a period of time, meditation develops a tremendous tenderness of heart...a softening of the mind and heart takes place that transforms the way we relate to ourselves and to others. We begin to feel more deeply and this depth of feeling becomes the wellspring of compassion.[176] Ken Wilber, the American author who speaks about Buddhist meditation in his book *Grace and Grit*, says that selfless service, social concern and mercy and compassion to others are the fruits of the practice of meditation.[177]

Contemplation and lived prayer

Richard J. Foster, in his book *Prayer: Finding the Heart's True Home*, writes:

> Each activity of daily life in which we stretch ourselves on behalf of others is *prayer* in *action* – the times when we scrimp and save in order to get the children something special; the times when we share our car with others on rainy mornings, leaving early to get them to work on time; the times when we keep up correspondence with friends or answer one last telephone call when we are dead tired at night. These times and many more like them are *lived* prayer.[178]

James Douglass, a pacifist writer, once described the essential unity of contemplation and action in terms of the great Chinese symbol of yin and yang. An ancient Chinese character for *yin* was a cloud (contemplative prayer); the symbol for *yang* was a banner waving in the breeze (action).

A balance between meditation and action

A life of meditation presupposes justice and compassion for others. Our social concern for justice and compassion will inevitably keep us on the path of meditation. However, some social activists may be tempted to neglect the interior life and thus open themselves to frustration and burnout. We all need to find a balance between meditation and action.

Meister Eckhart, the great medieval teacher of prayer, also warns meditators about divorcing themselves from the world around them. He says that once we find silence, we must not ignore our day-to-day affairs and responsibilities. Eckhart reminds us that the external world also is real and has its rights.

John Main on prayer and action

John Main felt quite strongly about the close connection between meditation and action in our lives. He says:

> It often seems to many people that prayer is an introspective state and that the meditator is someone going into oneself to the exclusion of people and creation around them. Nothing could be further from the truth.... Because meditation leads us into the actual experience of love at the centre of our being, it necessarily makes us more loving people in our ordinary lives and relationships.[179]

Action springs from and is grounded in contemplation

In his 200 recorded talks on the subject of contemplative prayer, John Main has a recurring theme that the daily practice of meditation necessarily makes us more loving people in our everyday lives and relationships. He knew that the teaching and experience through the ages of those who pray in silence is that this way of prayer is the springboard that launches us into fruitful action. In the book *The Way of Unknowing* he says:

> If our life is rooted in Christ, rooted in his love and the conscious knowledge of his love, then we need have no anxiety about regulating our action. Our action will always spring from and be informed and shaped by that love. Indeed, the more active we are, the more important it is that our action springs from and is grounded in contemplation. And contemplation means deep, silent, communion: knowing who we are. Knowing who we are by being who we are; that we are rooted and founded in Christ.[180]

Prayer and action: both sides of the same coin

Our prayer life and our actions cannot be separated, for they are two sides of the same coin. As we have seen, this mixed life of prayer and action, was chosen by Jesus himself, who taught and preached and healed while at the same time devoting so much time to prayer.

For all of us who meditate, it is important to remember that we cannot enjoy the silence and stillness while ignoring our worldly or family affairs and responsibilities. That would simply be a delusion. On the other hand, meditation will give us the spiritual energy to change the world. The great 17th-century spiritual guide Father Louis Lallemant said that a person who prays will accomplish more in one year than a person who does not pray will accomplish in an entire lifetime.

Henri Nouwen on social activism

The late Henri Nouwen, Catholic priest, writer and social critic, believed passionately in social issues and was particularly involved in liberation theology in South America. Born in Holland, he taught at a number of prestigious American universities, including Yale, Harvard and Notre Dame. He was the author of over 25 books, and from 1986 on spent the last years of his life at Daybreak, a L'Arche home for people with developmental disabilities in Richmond Hill, Ontario, Canada.

Nouwen, despite his own active life, pointed out that we must beware of being carried away by frenetic activism. He emphasizes that grounding ourselves in God's love and a disciplined life of prayer is a prerequisite before we jump into every new cause and issue. He writes that "dealing with burning issues without being rooted in a deep personal relationship with God easily leads to divisiveness"; I would also add that it leads to burnout."

The inner eye of love

In meditation there is an awakening of the inner eye, the eye of the heart, the inner eye of love. This is the *metanoia* or conversion that is beautifully described in Ezekiel (36:26-27). "A new heart I will give you and a new spirit I will put within you; and I will take out of your flesh the heart of stone...and I will put my spirit within you." This is the gospel cry of Jesus: "Change your hearts, for the kingdom of heaven is at hand" (Matthew 3:2). On the journey of meditation, the inner eye of love transforms our hearts and leads us into a life of fruitful action. For without prayer our actions can often be very sterile. Perhaps St. Teresa of Avila said it most succinctly: "This is the reason for prayer, my daughters, the birth always of good works, good works." Meditation will never lead us into a selfish preoccupation with ourselves.

QUESTION 50

Q. I've been deeply wounded emotionally from childhood trauma. Is there such a thing as inner healing on the path of Christian Meditation? How does this work? How does one achieve closure? Does it serve the same function as going to a psychotherapist?

A. Perhaps I should start off with a beautiful quotation from St. John of the Cross:

> Interior silence, the inner stillness to which meditation leads, is where the Spirit secretly anoints the soul and heals our deepest wounds.[181]

Yes, we realize today, through the social sciences and a better psychological understanding of what makes us tick, that many of us are emotionally wounded to some extent, that many of us have repressed feelings that often go back to infancy.

Where do crippling feelings come from?

In fact, psychologists speculate today that some of these repressed feelings can go right back to the womb. Even before birth we are subject to the emotional stress of our mother, especially her fears and anxieties.

In early childhood, many of us were deprived of the warm affection and acceptance of parents and siblings. We bury this painful memory and anger in our unconscious. Childhood abuse by parents and others is another serious wound that is often repressed into the unconscious. We may not remember some of these events of childhood, but the emotions do remember. Later in life, we often wonder where the force of these crippling feelings is coming from.

"Emotional junk" from early childhood

Most of us have a heavy burden of "emotional junk" accumulated from early childhood. The body and the unconscious mind are the storehouse for this undigested emotional garbage. These often crushing, painful memories can cripple us in body, mind and spirit unless they are somehow released to the conscious level.

We now know that people can grow up intellectually and physically while their emotional lives remain at the level of infancy. This happens because they have never been able to integrate their repressed childhood emotions with their adult selves. Unless there is a healing and they have made peace with their past, they are not able to relate in a healthy way in their current and future relationships.[182]

On meeting dependency needs

Children who are deprived of affection, for instance, may later choose spouses who they think can meet this dependency need. A marriage is usually headed for serious trouble if a man chooses a mother instead of a wife, or a woman chooses a father instead of a husband. People who are emotionally dependent can also find themselves in a marriage where they desire closeness but are still emotionally unavailable and distant towards their partner.

Wounds in the psyche must be released from our unconscious

Some people have a deep hatred of their mother or father. They harbour deep resentment arising from neglect, maltreatment and sometimes sexual abuse. These are wounds in the psyche and they continue to afflict us unless they are released from our unconscious. People who came from an abused, neglected or emotionally bankrupt family often suffer from depression, anxiety and fear of trusting others in their adult lives. They often have low self-esteem, and frequently view themselves as unlovable. They desire closeness but often keep people at a distance. Today we are recognizing more and more some of the terrible effects of emotional or physical abuse that children suffer in infancy and early childhood.

Well, what is the relationship between this kind of woundedness and the silence and stillness of Christian meditation? I'd like to tell you a story that dramatically makes the connection.

Galilee House in Ireland

A few years ago I visited a rehabilitation centre called Galilee House in County Kildare, Ireland, which was then run by a Catholic priest, Father Pat Murray. Father Pat spent seven months with John Main at the Montreal Benedictine Priory in 1981 to 1982. Galilee House is a house of healing growth and prayer.

The aim of Galilee House is to rehabilitate the most wounded people in Ireland: drug addicts, alcoholics, people in severe depression, victims of childhood abuse, and many who have simply buried anger, anxiety and resentment in their unconscious. Galilee House has had wonderful success over the years in healing these men and women and returning them to normal life in Irish society.

Psychotherapy and meditation

Participants in this intensive program at my visit were offered a group session of psychotherapy each day, but in addition they meditated in silence twice daily and listened to two talks each day (14 talks per week) by John Main. At the house I visited in County Kildare, there was a meditation room with 40 meditation stools; on the wall, engraved in copper, is John Main's advice on how to meditate.

While visiting, I asked Father Pat the reason for the great success rate of the Galilee House program. He pointed out that most of the people referred to Galilee House had suppressed anger or buried resentment and had often suffered a lack of forgiveness in their lives – neuroses and hurts, said Pat, that had generally existed in their unconscious since early childhood. Many had suffered childhood abuse.

Quite often, he pointed out, these wounds go back to a neurotic relationship with one's parents that, unfortunately, can cripple us emotionally.

Saying the mantra and healing

Now what is the process that leads to this inner healing, the healing of the wounded sensibility, the healing of hurts? As Father Pat pointed out, it is simply saying our mantra in meditation that opens us to the healing of love. In the silence of meditation, God reaches down into the depths and liberates us little by little from the emotional damage of a lifetime. There is an organic unfolding of our buried neuroses in their own time.

Father Pat was unequivocal that, while the psychotherapy provided is somewhat helpful, the real reason why patients healed in the Galilee program is meditation. He put it succinctly: "When people come into contact with *the* healer they begin to heal." He explained further that "in the silence of meditation, God who is love penetrates to the buried unconscious, allowing the suppressed anger and fear to surface and to be healed." "Exposed to the light," he continued, "neuroses begin to melt away." The healing power of Christ, he said, drains the poisoned memories away.

The first great key to healing

He was quick to point out that meditation doesn't wipe out the memory. Rather, the memory loses its power over us. Once these memories have been identified and brought to the light, he said, Christ frees us from the crippling effects of what we had buried in our unconscious and we begin an inner healing. He added, "In meditation, we come to accept ourselves as we are. And this self-acceptance is the first great key to healing."

In meditation, he continued, we come to an experiential conviction that we are loved by another person, profoundly loved. We understand deeply that it is not that I love, but that *I am loved.*

God puts his finger on our wounds

Through this acceptance of the gift of love, we grow from childhood to adulthood. In this healing process of meditation, as Father Pat said, our pain is identified and brought into the light, and neuroses and hang-ups of all kinds melt away. In meditation our conscious level is swept clean. With incredible accuracy God puts his finger on exactly the spot, the wound, the unconscious memory that needs attention.

It's interesting that the word "meditation" and the word "medicine" come from the same root. Medicine means that which heals the physical; meditation means that which heals the spiritual. Both have healing power. To be healed simply means to be made whole.

The great healer is love

In this healing we face up to the truth about ourselves; the truth will make us free. We also come to understand ourselves. Psychologists agree that understanding is immensely healing. When I come to understand myself, my childhood relationship with my parents or with my family environment, a great measure of healing is already accomplished. The next step is forgiveness.

The need to forgive

The other great key to healing, says Father Pat, is forgiveness. In meditation we seem to be given the grace and strength to forgive those who have hurt us. However, forgiveness is also a gift we have to give ourselves. There is a story of a former inmate of a Nazi concentration camp visiting a friend who had shared this ordeal with him.

"Have you forgiven the Nazis?" he asked his friend.

"Yes."

"Well, I haven't. I'm still consumed with hatred for them," the first man declared.

"In that case," said his friend gently, "they still have you in prison."[183]

This story makes a vital point. Bitterness and anger imprison us emotionally. Forgiveness sets us free.

But forgiveness is not enough in itself to accomplish healing. The great healer is *love*. Ultimately, healing comes through faith in Christ.

Don't fight the process

When the fears and anxieties, hurts and pains that we repressed since childhood start to come up in meditation, what do we do? The answer is this: "We do nothing, just *be*." We simply let the debris from the unconscious come to the surface. Don't fight this process. Accept it. Let the process take place. At the time of meditation, these repressed feelings and memories are distractions; the universal way to handle distractions is to return to the recitation of the mantra.

As mentioned, in the normal course of events, God's presence in our daily practice of meditation will heal our childhood memories. However, in answer to your question, in some cases, a friend, a counsellor, a member of a meditation group, or perhaps a psychotherapist, may be needed to assist one through a particular crisis during the healing process.

Our shadow side begins to heal

To sum up, in the regular daily practice of Christian Meditation, the deep rest and silence created by our mantra in addition to God's action loosens up the emotional memories of childhood. The shadow side of the psyche begins to heal. None of us comes to meditation with a clean slate. So for all of us, one aspect of our spiritual journey is this struggle with the buried unconscious. We are all wounded in one way or another. We all need healing. In meditation we come from brokenness to wholeness.

Meditation propels us into greater wholeness

In his book *The Present Christ*, John Main points out that the healing aspects of meditation go beyond our woundedness:

> Meditation does restore us to a deeper harmony of body and spirit, but it always remains an essentially spiritual growth. All growth is a form of healing. Not just a retrospective healing of past wounds but it propels the whole person we are now into greater wholeness, the health we are created for. And so we can say that meditation is a growth beyond limitations.[184]

QUESTION 51

Q. What is the role of the weekly Christian Meditation group? Why should meditators meet together? Where do they meet? What happens at the weekly meetings? How would one start a new group?

A. It has been said that in each age God raises up prophets and teachers to ensure that his work is carried on. John Main is certainly regarded as one of the great spiritual teachers of the 20th century, but in a real sense he was also a prophet. John Main had a deep insight and prophetic vision that his teaching on silence and stillness in prayer would primarily be handed down in small groups. It was his hope that this teaching and practice would be shared in an organic way through support groups of men and women meeting weekly in homes, churches, schools and workplaces. He had a profound understanding of the ancient tradition of Christians gathering together to pray.

Meditation groups: communities of faith

As Laurence Freeman points out, "John Main saw this modern development of contemplation as originating in the communities of faith and the liturgy of the heart of the early church. These early Christians also gathered in small groups in one another's houses. This coming together in prayer formed the *koinonia*, or the social interaction and communion, that was the distinguishing mark and power of the early church." These small groups met to pray and offer support and encouragement to each other in their common faith.

Support on the common pilgrimage

There is no doubt that the teaching of spirituality is historically rooted in the tradition of the small group. The Israelites were divided up into small tribes and close family units, particularly during their sojourn in the wilderness. Jesus chose a small group of 12 to form the heart of his ministry. Throughout the last 2000 years, small groups of men and women have banded together in the monastic life to live in community and support each other on the spiritual journey. It seems only natural that people who are praying contemplatively in the 21st century should also come together in groups to support each other on their common pilgrimage.

Small groups are redefining spirituality

A recent book, *Sharing the Journey* by Robert Wuthnow,[185] documents the growing popularity and influence of small groups in creating community and teaching spirituality. Wuthnow maintains that small groups "may be redefining spirituality" and that the church is once again becoming alive in the humble homes of those on the spiritual path. The author also confirms through research that small groups have emerged in response to the impersonalization of society and the weakening of family and community ties.

What has experience taught us over the years since John Main started the first Christian Meditation group at Ealing Abbey in London in 1975? Here is what we have learned about the role of the weekly meditation group.

Why meditators meet in groups

The heart of the meditation group is the sharing of silence together. This is the primary reason why people around the world are spontaneously starting small groups to meditate weekly together. The power and strength of meditating together comes from the words of Jesus: "Where two or three are gathered in my name, there I am in the midst of them" (Matthew 18:20). This is the foremost reason for getting together once a week. It is as if meditators instinctively realize that this is a journey that is difficult to make alone; it is a journey that is so much easier if we make it with others. It is true that no one else can meditate for us, that we meditate by ourselves each day, but at the same time we realize that we need the support of others if we are to persevere on this journey.

A spiritual bond develops among members

Meeting in a group promotes a spiritual bond among the members and a mutual concern between those who have set out on a common pilgrimage. The meditation group is really a community of faith, much like the early Christians experienced community in St. Paul's time.

The group setting enables beginners to learn how to meditate. Newcomers can be integrated into a group at any time. Experience has shown that when a group starts in a new geographic area, people who have never meditated before will join the group. New groups introduce new meditators to the teaching.

Support and encouragement on the path

The weekly group meeting provides support and encouragement to those who might be discouraged or experiencing difficulties on the path. All of us need, from time to time, the encouragement of seeing others who are faithful and committed to the discipline.

We also need to absorb the teaching more deeply. We do so at the weekly meeting by listening to a recorded talk by John Main on some aspect of Christian Meditation. There are 200 talks by Father John and additional talks by Laurence Freeman available on various aspects of meditation. These talks give instruction, deepen our motivation, and help us to persevere on the path. They give us a spiritual boost each week; they are part of the food we need for the journey.

The question and answer period at the end of the meeting often helps immeasurably in clarifying situations, not only for the questioner but also for other members of the group. Discussion allows members to express their doubts, fears and misunderstandings of the teaching.[186]

Where do groups meet?

Groups meet in diverse locations and at various hours throughout the day and evening. There are now over 1200 groups meeting in 48 countries around the world in homes, apartments, schools, churches, rectories, religious communities, Christian Meditation centres, chapels, universities, prisons, government office buildings, a department store, senior citizens' homes and factories.

Lists of groups and meeting times are available from Christian Meditation group leaders in various countries. An international list of groups is available from The International Centre, The World Community for Christian Meditation, St Mark's Church, Myddleton Square, London EC1 R1XX England.

What happens at the weekly meeting?

The typical weekly group meeting lasts about one hour and includes an opening welcome to the members by the group leader. Many groups light a candle to symbolize the presence of Christ. This is followed by the playing of an audiocassette by John Main on some aspect of the practice and teaching of meditation. Then the heart of the meeting – 25 minutes of silent meditation – begins. At the conclusion of meditation, announcements can be made and newcomers are given a chance to ask questions pertaining to the teaching. In some groups the meditation group leader may give a five-minute talk relating to John Main's talk that evening.

On starting a group

How do groups start? The most important ingredient in starting a new group is the commitment of a leader to the time and effort required to set up and guide a group. A decision must be made about the time and day of the meeting and a (preferably quiet) location must be found. A number of things can be done to attract newcomers to the group. A letter can be sent to all churches in the area asking for pulpit and bulletin announcements about the new group. Posters can be produced for church bulletin boards. Notices can be sent to religious, daily, weekly or community newspapers. An announcement can be sent to local cablevision TV stations and radio stations. Notices can be pinned on shopping mall bulletin boards.

The role of the leader

The leader must work at setting up the group as if everything depended on himself or herself, while at the same time realizing that in the dimension of faith, the growth and success of the group will depend on God. Numbers are unimportant in a group. Our Lord said, "Where two or three are gathered, in my name, there I am in the midst of them." Where two meditators are gathered there is a meditation group. Once a group starts, others will join in time.

A leader will require a cassette player, some of John Main's audiocassettes on meditation, and a timer. Many group leaders use a pre-programmed cassette timing tape containing a few moments of music, 25 minutes of silence, and a few moments of music to signal the end of the meditation period. But more than these material items, the meditation leader will require faith and commitment – faith to "wait on the Lord" not only in meditation, but also for an increase in new members. God works through the instrument of human beings. If the leader has worked to communicate information about the new group, God will bring more members, and a new meditation group will be born and will flourish.

What are the advantages of small groups?

- Small Christian Meditation groups have a great advantage in adapting to their environment. They require virtually no resources other than the time their members devote to them each week, and they can be started with relative ease.

- The small group provides a sense of community for people who feel the loss and breakdown of neighbourhoods and personal family ties, and support and sharing for those who need encouragement.

- We all need the affirmation of others, and thus our faith can be strengthened through the bonds of love, caring and fellowship that develop in the small group. Basic spiritual and human values are shared in a group setting and friendships develop.

- Contrary to public perception, we are not a society of rugged individualists who wish to go it entirely alone, but rather a communal people capable of banding together in groups for mutual support.[187]

The spiritual revolution taking place today

While these findings will be of interest to anyone participating in Christian Meditation groups, either as members or leaders, it should be pointed out that the period of meditation itself will provide a strong bond of unity within the group. Because it is the prayer of Jesus himself, it necessarily follows that a spirit of love and friendship will develop within the group.

As Laurence Freeman has written: "The early Christians experienced this inner reality of prayer and knew the strong bond of unity it gave. But as the church grew older, its emphasis fell more and more upon formal prayer and external observance. Its interiority weakened, and wherever it weakened, the church's influence diminished and her spiritual life grew more sterile."[188] Today in the small group setting we are recapturing a prayer that leads us from the head to the heart, from fragmentation to unity, from isolation to caring. This is the spiritual revolution taking place around the world today.

QUESTION 52

Q. What is the relationship between *lectio divina* and contemplative prayer?

A. *Lectio divina*, which means "divine reading," was originally a Benedictine monastic spiritual practice. It has often been interpreted to mean "the slow, prayerful and loving reading of Scripture." It is a spiritual practice of reflecting on the word of God, giving it our attention and using our faculties to give deep consideration to the text. Some authors say that "we chew on the word of God" or "mull over the word of God."

Lectio: the door to contemplation

The practice of *lectio*, in which one ponders the "heart" of the text, frequently leads to a state of consciousness where we simply remain silent in the presence of God, beyond words and thoughts and reading. It often leads to a "resting in God." It has also been called listening with the heart. So *lectio* can be an ideal preparation for the silence and stillness of contemplative prayer. The two go hand in hand. The early monks felt *lectio* was the door that opened a monk to the contemplative experience.

From the written word to resting in the Lord

In the monastic tradition, *lectio divina*, or the reflective reading of, listening to and digesting of Scripture, was seen as an integral part of the monk's spiritual development. *Lectio divina* was meant to lead a monk from the written word to "resting" in the Lord. To some extent this tradition has been lost in monastic communities. This is why John Main felt that a return to the prayerful reading of Scripture was a necessary complement to the mantra in preparation for bringing one to the interior silence of meditation.

To let ourselves be read by God

The late priest and writer Henri Nouwen expanded the definition of *lectio divina* to include any spiritual reading that is "read with a desire to let God come closer to us." The purpose of this kind of spiritual reading, says Nouwen, is not to master knowledge or information, but to let God's spirit master us. Strange as it may sound, he says, this kind of spiritual reading means to let ourselves be read by God. This is Nouwen's updated interpretation of *lectio divina*.

QUESTION 53

Q. Is there a special call to this way of prayer, or is everybody invited?

A. I suggest the answer is yes to both of these questions. Karl Rahner, the great 20th-century theologian, was adamant that contemplative prayer "is not confined to a privileged few" but is a universal call to each and every Christian. He also added that this way of prayer "occurs within the framework of normal graces."[189]

The contemplative call originates with our baptism

Thomas Merton insisted that the fall from paradise in Genesis was a fall from the contemplative state and a loss of the original unity with God. For that reason Merton came to realize that contemplation was not a call to a chosen few, but a universal call to everyone. He believed that the contemplative call for Christians originated with our baptism, and expressed sorrow that so few Christians answer this call from God to contemplative prayer. In *What Is Contemplation?* Merton writes:

> The seeds of contemplation are planted in every Christian soul at Baptism. But seeds must grow and develop before you reap the harvest. There are thousands of Christians walking about the face of the earth bearing in their bodies the infinite God of whom they know practically nothing. The seeds of contemplation have been planted in these souls, but they merely lie dormant. They do not germinate.[190]

The seeds of contemplation

Regarding those who reject the contemplative call, Merton elaborates on the gospel story of the sower who scatters the seeds: some seeds fall in the path and are eaten up by the birds of the air; other seeds fall in shallow ground, do not take root, wither and die; but other seeds fall on fertile ground and bear fruit in due season. Merton points out that excessive activity, cares and concerns of the world often drown out the voice of God calling us to this way of prayer. In our excessive busyness, the seeds (God's call) are eaten up by the birds of the air or fall on infertile ground.

The heights of contemplation are offered to ordinary people

We must also remember that *The Cloud of Unknowing* says that this way of silent prayer is open to even the most unlearned person; the author adds that this prayer is simply a normal development of the ordinary Christian life. (See Question 34 on *The Cloud of Unknowing*.) Two other great medieval spiritual teachers, Meister Eckhart and Johannes Tauler, also reflect a similar teaching, that the heights of contemplative prayer are offered to ordinary people.

The Hound of Heaven chases us

While the invitation to the spiritual path and this way of prayer is open to every Christian, we also seem to receive an individual invitation. Perhaps this is best reflected in the poem "The Hound of Heaven" by Francis Thompson, where the Lord is portrayed as a bloodhound on the trail of each one of us (our special invitation). We do everything to block the invitation, but the Hound keeps chasing us:

> I fled Him, down the nights and down the days;
> I fled Him, down the arches of the years;
> I fled Him, down the labyrinthine ways
> Of my own mind; and in the midst of tears
> I hid from Him, and under running laughter.
>
> ....
>
> Still with unhurrying chase,
> And unperturbed pace,
> Deliberate speed, majestic instancy,
> Came on the following feet,

And a voice above their beat –
"Naught shelters thee, who wilt not shelter me."

At the end of the poem, Francis Thompson talks about how the Hound of Heaven has finally caught up with him. God speaks:

All which I took from thee I did but take
Not for thy harms,
But that thou might'st seek it in my arms.
All which thy child's mistake
Fancies as lost, I have stored for thee at home.[191]

If today you hear his voice, harden not your hearts

As the poem illustrates so well, it is Jesus who takes the initiative in our spiritual conversion, and it is Jesus who issues the invitation to a deeper way of prayer. In fact, many of those who are now meditating talk about receiving a double invitation. There seem to be two knocks on the door for many people: "Behold, I stand at the door and knock" (Revelation 3:20). It would seem that for some people, God issues a double invitation to this path of Christian Meditation.

So the call to contemplative prayer is a general call to everyone through our baptism. The seeds of contemplation are planted deeply with us. However, God also issues a unique call to each one of us. Thomas Merton put it well: "We become contemplative when God discovers Himself in us." We must always remember that the call to meditation is a gift and a grace from God: "If today you hear his voice, harden not your hearts" (Psalm 95:8).

QUESTION 54

Q. What is discursive meditation? How does it relate to the contemplative tradition of meditation?

A. Discursive meditation is a component of the Spiritual Exercises of the Society of Jesus (Jesuits). It is a form of analytical mental prayer employing one's memory, imagination, intellect, will, and powers of reflection.

While the founder of the Jesuits, Ignatius of Loyola (1491–1556), wrote the Spiritual Exercises, the practice of discursive meditation developed in the Jesuits only in the years after the death of Ignatius. In the past two centuries, this form of prayer was consistent with the rationalistic worldview that formed the content of Western civilization as well as the content of the Roman Catholic Church. It was advocated by spiritual writers such as Tanquery, whose teachings on asceticism and spirituality were part of almost every seminary formation program.

Discursive meditation a preliminary step

Many experts, including the Jesuit author and teacher of prayer Father William Johnston, insist that Ignatius was a contemplative. Father Johnston feels that the later development of discursive meditation among the Jesuits was meant to be preparatory to silence and stillness in contemplative prayer. He feels that eventually prayer must proceed from the head to the heart and beyond words, memory and imagination.

A sure sign that we are meant to pray contemplatively is when discursive meditation forces us to throw up our hands in despair, when this head-centred approach to prayer simply causes frustration and we are convinced we can no longer pray at all. This is a sure sign that we are called to "rest in God" in silence and stillness and to heed the guidance of the Spirit leading us to a deeper way of prayer. Discursive meditation is generally thought of as a preliminary step to contemplative prayer.

Going beyond images, concepts and reasoning

We simply cannot grasp God through images, concepts or discursive reasoning. In Buddhism there is a saying: "If you see the Buddha, kill him." What this means is that whatever image or idea one has of Buddha, it is false.

Christians realize that our finite minds cannot grasp the infinity of God. When referring to the absolute, Hindus say God is not this (*neti*) and not that (*neti*).

In contemplative prayer, one goes beyond discursive images, concepts and thoughts in order to be united to God at a deeper level of one's being. It's not that images and concepts are false, but in contemplative prayer we descend to a deeper level of our psyche that opens us up to direct contact with God, to his knowledge and to his love.

QUESTION 55

Q. What if I fall asleep during meditation?

A. First, don't feel guilty about falling asleep. God loves us asleep or awake. The very fact that we are sitting to meditate is a sign that we are at least *open* to silence and God's presence. The problem of sleepiness can be bothersome to a small minority of meditators, but it can also be reassuring. It tells us that our nervous system and the chattering monkeys in our mind have begun to slow down.

How to deal with the problem

Let's deal with the problem. In meditation we are trying to do two very opposite things: be alert and yet, at the same time, be relaxed. When we doze off, the relaxation aspect of meditation has taken over from our alertness and concentration. Usually this happens when we are beginning the path of meditation. As we persevere in the discipline and grow in attention to saying the mantra and listening to the *sound* of the mantra, wakefulness deepens with the silence, and there is less of a tendency to doze off.

Causes of sleepiness

Sleeping during meditation can have several causes. We need to ask ourselves a few questions: Did I get enough sleep last night? Am I meditating late in the evening when I may be extremely tired? Am I meditating after drinking alcohol? Am I meditating too soon after a heavy meal? The digestion of food slows down our brain waves and metabolism. This leads to a lack of wakeful attention to the mantra and dozing off. It is best to meditate before a meal or, if this is not possible, to wait at least one hour after a meal before meditating.

Check your posture and breathing. (See Questions 10 and 12 on posture and breathing.)

One way to counteract sleepiness is to splash cold water on your face; even take a quick bath or shower before meditation. At times, though, you will need to dispel drowsiness and make a real effort to be alert. When you feel a doze coming on, check your posture and breathing and make a conscious effort to deal with the problem.

But one must not feel guilty about falling asleep. Again, God is present in sleep as in waking. Our role is simply to make the effort to stay awake and remember the words of Jesus to his disciples, "Could you not watch one hour with me?" (Mark 14:37).

QUESTION 56

Q. Is there an international centre that co-ordinates Christian Meditation groups around the world? Are there North American centres? Is there a Christian Meditation Web site?

A. Yes, there is an International Centre in London, England, part of the World Community for Christian Meditation (WCCM). There are now over 1200 Christian Meditation groups in 48 countries of the world associated with the WCCM. An international directory of the groups is maintained at the London centre. A guiding board oversees the direction of the Community, a quarterly newsletter, an annual John Main Seminar, and a School for Teachers program.

The address of the London Centre is:

Christian Meditation International Centre
St Mark's Church, Myddleton Square
London EC1 R1XX U.K.
Tel: 44 (0) 20 7278-2070
Fax: 44 (0) 20 7713-6346
E-mail: wccm@compuserve.com

In Canada, Christian Meditation books, tapes and resource material can be ordered from:

Christian Meditation Community
Canadian National Resource Centre
7211 Somerled Ave.
Montreal, QC H4V 1W9
Tel: 514-487-5569
Fax: 514-489-9899

In the United States, contact:

Christian Meditation Centre
193 Wilton Road West
Ridgefield, CT 06877
Tel: 203-438-2440
E-mail: pgulick@cwix.com

Information that will assist people in learning to meditate and to continue to meditate can be obtained from:

The John Main Centre
Box 56131
Ottawa, ON K1R 7Z0
Tel: 613-236-9437
Fax: 613-236-2821

Visit an extensive Christian Meditation Web site at www.wccm.org

This Web site includes the latest worldwide Christian Meditation news, coming events, available books, tapes and a chat line.

NOTES

[1]   *Community of Love* by John Main (Darton, Longman and Todd, 1990)

[2]   *Meister Eckhart: A Modern Translation* by Raymond B. Blakney (Harper and Row, 1941)

[3]   *The Way of Unknowing* by John Main (Darton, Longman and Todd, 1989)

[4]   *The Cloud of Unknowing,* edited by William Johnston (Doubleday Image Book, 1973)

[5]   *Ibid.*

[6]   *Moment of Christ* by John Main (Darton, Longman and Todd, 1984)

[7]   The term "The Cloud of Unknowing" refers to the presence of God; the author takes this term from the transfiguration where God appears in a cloud.

[8]   *The Cloud of Unknowing, edited by William Johnston* (Doubleday Image Book, 1973)

[9]   *Blue Mountain, a Journal for Spiritual Living* and the Newsletter of the Blue Mountain Centre of Meditation, Volume 11, Number 3, Tomales, Calif., USA

[10]   *New Scientist Magazine*, Aug. 21, 1986

[11]   *Study on Meditation and Tooth Decay* by Dr. Donald Morse, Director of Research, Temple University Department of Endodontology

[12]   Excerpts from *Christian Meditation: Contemplative Prayer for a New Generation* by Paul Harris (Darton, Longman and Todd, 1996)

[13]   *The Sacred World of the Christian* by Mary Anthony Wagner (The Liturgical Press, 1993)

[14]   Excerpts from *Christian Meditation: Contemplative Prayer for a New Generation* by Paul Harris (Darton, Longman and Todd and Novalis, 1996)

[15]   *The Wisdom of the Desert* by Thomas Merton (New Directions, 1960)

[16]   *The Contemplative Life* by Thomas Philippe OP (Crossroad, 1990)

[17]   From *The Art of Prayer: An Orthodox Anthology* (Faber and Faber, 1966)

[18]   *The Collected Works of St. Teresa of Avila* (Institute of Carmelite Studies, 1985)

[19]   *Seeds of Contemplation* by Thomas Merton (New Directions, 1949) [author's italics]

20   *The Unstruck Bell* by Eknath Easwaran (Nilgiri Press, 1977)

21   *Moment of Christ* by John Main (Darton, Longman and Todd, 1984)

22   *I am Awake: Discovering Prayer* by Stephen J. Rossetti (Paulist Press, 1987)

23   *Seasons of Your Heart: Prayer and Reflections* by Macrina Wiederkehr (Harper Collins, 1992)

24   *English Writings of Richard Rolle, Hermit of Hampole*, edited by Hope Emily Allen (St. Clair Shores, MI: Scholarly, 1971)

25   *On Prayer* by Evagrius Pontus [The Philokelia] (Faber and Faber, 1951)

26   *Silence and Stillness in Every Season: Daily Readings with John Main*, edited by Paul Harris (Darton, Longman and Todd and Continuum, 1997)

27   Excerpts from *Christian Meditation: Contemplative Prayer for a New Generation* by Paul Harris (Darton, Longman and Todd and Novalis, 1996)

28   Excerpts from *Christian Meditation: Contemplative Prayer for a New Generation* by Paul Harris (Darton, Longman and Todd and Novalis, 1996)

29   *Christian Meditation: Contemplative Prayer for a New Generation* (Darton, Longman and Todd and Novalis, 1996)

30   *Word Into Silence* by John Main (Darton, Longman and Todd, 1980)

31   *What is Contemplation* by Thomas Merton (Templegate, 1978)

32   *A Tree Full of Angels* by Macrina Wiederkehr (Harper Collins. 1988)

33   Excerpts from *Christian Meditation: Contemplative Prayer for a New Generation* by Paul Harris (Darton, Longman and Todd and Novalis, 1996)

34   *The Way of Chuang Tzu*, translated by Thomas Merton (New Directions, 1965)

35   *The Complete Works of John of the Cross* (Institute of Carmelite Studies, 1974)

36   *Ibid.*

37   *The Present Christ* by John Main (Darton, Longman and Todd, 1985)

38   Quoted in *Living from Within* by Philippa Craig (a UK Grail Publication)

39   *The Tempo of Modern Life* by James Truslow, quoted in *The Readers Digest*

40   *The Complete Works of St. John of the Cross, Doctor of the Church* (Burns, Oates, 1943)

[41]   *Tao Te Ching* by Lao-Tzu, translated by Stephen Mitchell (Harper Collins, 1988)

[42]   *Born Contemplative: Introducing Children to Meditation* by Madeleine Simon (Darton, Longman and Todd, 1993) [author's italics]

[43]   *Evagrius Ponticus, The Praktikos, Chapters on Prayer* by John Eudes Bamberger (Cistercian Publications, 1970)

[44]   *Confessions of St. Augustine* (Doubleday, 1960)

[45]   *Word Into Silence* by John Main (Darton, Longman and Todd, 1980)

[46]   *Wisdom of the Desert* by Thomas Merton (New Directions, 1960)

[47]   Quoted in *Man's Search for Meaning* by Viktor E. Frankl (Washington Square Press, 1963)

[48]   *The Heart of Silence: Contemplative Prayer by Those Who Practice it* by Paul Harris (Darton, Longman and Todd and Novalis, 1999)

[49]   *Treatises and Sermons of Meister Eckhart* (Octagon Books, 1983)

[50]   *Grace and Grit* by Ken Wilber (Shambala Publications, 1991)

[51]   *The Collected Works of John of the Cross* (Institute of Carmelite Studies, 1974)

[52]   *The Wisdom of the Desert* by Thomas Merton (New Directions, 1961)

[53]   *Morning Light* by Jean Sulivan (Paulist Press, 1988)

[54]   *The World of Silence* by Max Picard (H. Regnery, 1988)

[55]   *The Collected Works of St. John of the Cross* (Institute of Carmelite Studies, 1974)

[56]   *The Complete Poetical Works of Henry Wordsworth Longfellow* (Houghton, Mifflin, 1922)

[57]   *Treatises and Seminars of Meister Eckhart* (Octagon Books, 1983)

[58]   *Mother Teresa, Contemplative at the Heart of the World* edited by Brother Angelo Devannanda (Fount, Harper, Collins, 1988)

[59]   *Molchanie: The Silence of God* by Catherine De Hueck Doherty (Madonna House Publications, 1991)

[60]   *Word Into Silence* by John Main (Darton, Longman and Todd, 1980)

[61]   *The Little Prince* by Antoine de Saint-Exupery (Harcourt Brace, 1943)

[62]   *Confessions of St. Augustine* (Doubleday, 1960)

63   *The Door to Silence* by John Main (Communitas Tapes, The World Community for Christian Meditation)

64   *Thomas Merton's Dark Path: The Inner Experience of a Contemplative* by William H. Shannon (Farrar, Strauss and Giroux, 1981)

65   *The Collected Works of St. John of the Cross* (Institute of Carmelite Studies, 1974)

66   *Writings from the Philokalia on the Prayer of the Heart* (Faber and Faber, 1951)

67   *Christian Meditation: The Gethsemani Talks* (World Community for Christian Meditation, 1977)

68   *Being on the Way* by John Main (Communitas Tapes, World Community for Christian Meditation)

69   *Being in Love* by William Johnston (Collins, 1988)

70   *Word Made Flesh* by John Main (Darton, Longman and Todd, 1993)

71   *Meditation: Commonsense Directions for an Uncommon Life* by Eknath Eswaran (Nilgri Press, 1978)

72   *The Grounds of Reasons of Christian Regeneration* by William Law (James Darling, 1845)

73   *Swami Abhishiktananda: The Man and His Teachings* by Vandana Mataji (ISPCK, 1986)

74   Excerpts on this question are from *Christian Meditation: Contemplative Prayer for a New Generation* by Paul Harris (Darton, Longman and Todd and Novalis, 1996)

75   *Reconciled Being* by Mary McAleese (Medio-Media/Arthur James, 1997)

76   *John Main by Those Who Knew Him*, edited by Paul Harris (Darton, Longman and Todd and Novalis, 1991)

77   "Intercessory Prayer" by Fr. Patrick Eastman (*Monos*, September, October 2000, Tulsa, Oklahoma, USA)

78   *Prayer* by Abhishiktananda (ISPCK Publishers, 1967)

79   *Benedictine Monasticism* by Abbot Cuthbert Butler (Longman's, 1924)

80   *John Cassian Conferences* (The Classics of Western Spirituality, Paulist Press, 1985)

81   *Letters From the Heart* by John Main (The Crossroad Publishing Co., 1985)

[82] *The Jesus Prayer: Past and Present* by Stephen A. Kirkegaard, Master of Divinity Thesis, Trinity College, Toronto, 1993.

[83] *Fanny and Zooey* by J.D. Salinger (Little, Brown and Co., 1961)

[84] The quotations of Bishop Ware in this answer on the Jesus Prayer are taken from the article "The Power of the Name: The Function of the Jesus Prayer" in *Cross Currents* magazine, summer-fall, 1974

[85] St. Theophan The Recluse, cited in *The Art of Prayer*, translated by F. Kadloubovsky and E.M. Palmer (London, 1966)

[86] *The Cloud of Unknowing*, edited by William Johnston (Doubleday Image Books, 1973)

[87] *The Mysticism of the Cloud of Unknowing* by William Johnston (Anthony Clarke Books, 1978)

[88] Various sources on Julian date her death between 1416 and 1429. Because records were not kept, it is difficult to be sure of the date.

[89] I am deeply grateful for a number of insights into Julian's life by Julia Bolton Holloway, Hermit of the Holy Family and Librarian of Biblioteca Fioretta Mazzei, Florence, Italy. Her studies and scholarship on Julian's life can be found on the Web site http://www.umilta.net.

[90] There are a number of excellent translations of *The Revelations of Divine Love* including those by Clifton Walters (Penguin, 1966), James Walsh, S.J. (Anthony Clarke), and a new Penguin translation by Elizabeth Spearing. There have been six translations in the last 25 years.

[91] *Seeds of Destruction* by Thomas Merton (Farrar, Straus and Giroux, 1961)

[92] Conrad Pepler OP, *The English Religious Heritage* (London: Blackfriars, 1958)

[93] *Revelations of Divine Love* by Julian of Norwich, ch. 52 (New York: Penguin, 1966)

[94] *Meister Eckhart: A Modern Translation* by Raymond B. Blakney (Harper and Row, 1941)

[95] Writings from the Philokalia on *Prayer of the Heart* by E. Kadloubovsky and E.M. Palmer (Faber and Faber, 1984)

[96] *The Way of the Pilgrim* and *The Pilgrim Continues His Way*, translated by Helen Bacovcin (Doubleday Image Books, 1978)

[97] Jules Monachanin, *Mystique de l'Inde, Mystere Chretien*, (Fayard, 1974)

[98]   *Ascent to the Depth of the Heart: The Spiritual Diary 1948-73 of Swami Abhishiktananda* (ISPCK, 1998)

[99]   Most of the books have been published by the Indian publisher ISPCK, PO 1585, Kashmere Gate, Delhi 110 006, India

[100]   Letter to Sr. Marie Therese, Carmelite Sister in France

[101]   *Swami Abhishiktananda: The Man and His Teachings* (ISPCK ,1986)

[102]   *Ibid.*

[103]   *The Secret of Arunachala* by Swami Abhishiktananda (ISPCK, 1979)

[104]   *Ermite du Saccidanada* (Casterman, 1956)

[105]   *Swami Abhishiktananda: His Life Told Through His Letters* (ISPCK, 1989)

[106]   *Prayer by Abhishiktananda* (ISPCK, 1967)

[107]   *Ibid.*

[108]   *Ibid.*

[109]   *An Interrupted Life: The Diaries of Etty Hillesum* (Pantheon Books, 1981)

[110]   *Letters from Westerbork* by Etty Hillesum (Pantheon Books, 1986)

[111]   *Simone Weil, A Modern Pilgrimage*, by Robert Coles (Addison-Wesley, 1987)

[112]   *Waiting on God* by Simone Weil, translated by Emma Crawford (G.P. Putnam's Sons, 1951)

[113]   *The Simone Weil Reader* edited by George A. Panichos (David McKay, 1977)

[114]   *Waiting on God*, translated by Emma Crawford (G.P. Putnam's Sons, 1951)

[115]   *Ibid.*

[116]   *Simone Weil, A Modern Pilgrimage* by Robert Coles (Addison-Wesley, 1987)

[117]   *Mysticism* by Evelyn Underhill (Oneworld Publications, 1994)

[118]   *The Golden Sequence: a Four-Fold Study of the Spiritual Life*, talk given in 1930 and published in 1932 by Methuen and Harper and Row

[119]   *The Letters of Evelyn Underhill* edited by Charles Williams (Longmans Green and Co, 1943)

[120]   *Ibid.*

[121]   *In the Stillness Dancing* by Neil McKenty (Darton, Longmans and Todd, 1986)

[122]   *Christian Meditation: The Gethsemani Talks by John Main (World Community for Christian Meditation)*

[123]   *In the Stillness Dancing* by Neil McKenty (Darton, Longman and Todd, 1986)

[124]   "Merton and Main and the New Monasticism" by Gregory J. Ryan in *Monastic Studies*, Number 18, 1988

[125]   *Thoughts in Solitude* by Thomas Merton (Farrar, Strauss and Giroux, 1976)

[126]   *What is Contemplation* by Thomas Merton (Templegate, 1981)

[127]   From the poem *The Tears of the Blind Lion* by Thomas Merton (New Directions, 1949)

[128]   *The Ascent of Truth* by Thomas Merton (Harcourt Brace, 1981) [author's italics]

[129]   *Seeds of Contemplation* by Thomas Merton (New Directions, 1949)

[130]   *New Seeds of Contemplation* by Thomas Merton (New Directions, 1972)

[131]   *The Climate of Monastic Prayer* by Thomas Merton (Cistercian Studies Series, 1981)

[132]   Many of these stories are from the book *In the Stillness Dancing* by Neil McKenty (Darton, Longman and Todd, 1986)

[133]   *John Main by Those Who Knew Him*, edited by Paul Harris (Darton, Longman and Todd and Novalis, 1991)

[134]   *Christian Meditation: The Gethsemani Talks* (World Community for Christian Meditation, 1977)

[135]   *Ibid*. Swami Satyananda is quoting from the Indian Scriptures, The Upanishads.

[136]   *Christian Meditation: The Gethsemani Talks* (World Community for Christian Meditation, 1977)

[137]   Much of the material in response to this question has come from *John Main: A Biography in Text and Photos*, edited by Paul Harris (Medio-Media, 2001)

[138]   *The Golden String* by Bede Griffiths (Collins, Fount, 1984)

[139]   From the *Inner Directions Journal*, Summer 1996

[140]   *The Marriage of East and West* by Bede Griffiths (Collins, 1982)

[141]   *The New Creation in Christ* by Bede Griffiths (Darton, Longman and Todd, 1992)

[142]   Quoted in *Christian Meditation: Contemplative Prayer for a New Generation* by Paul Harris (Darton, Longman and Todd and Novalis, 1996)

[143]   Carlo Carretto, *Selected Writings*, edited by Robert Ellsberg (Orbis Books, 1994)

[144]   *Letters From the Desert* by Carlo Carretto (Orbis Books, 1972)

[145]   Carlo Carretto, *Selected Writings*, edited by Robert Ellsberg (Orbis Books, 1994)

[146]   *Letters to Dolcidia* by Carlo Carretto (Orbis Books, 1992)

[147]   *Letters From the Desert* by Carlo Carretto (Orbis Books, 1972)

[148]   *Ibid.*

[149]   *In Search of the Beyond* by Carlo Carretto (Orbis Books, 1975)

[150]   *The Desert in the City* by Carlo Carretto (Collins, 1979)

[151]   *Letters From the Desert* by Carlo Carretto (Orbis Books, 1972)

[152]   *Mother Teresa, Contemplative at the Heart of the World*, edited by Brother Angelo Devananda (Fount, Harper Collins, 1988)

[153]   *Ibid.*

[154]   *Ibid.*

[155]   *Prayer, Seeking the Heart of God*, Mother Teresa and Brother Roger (Fount, Harper Collins, 1992)

[156]   *Ibid.*

[157]   *Mother Teresa of Calcutta, The Love of Christ, Spiritual Counsels*, edited by Georges Gorree and Jean Barber (Harper and Row, 1982)

[158]   *Ibid.*

[159]   *Mother Teresa, Total Surrender*, edited by Brother Angelo Devananda (Servant Publications, 1985)

[160]   *Mother Teresa, Her People and Her Work* by Desmond Doig (Collins, 1976)

[161]   *Such a Vision of the Street, Mother Teresa, the Spirit and the Work* by Eileen Egan (Doubleday and Co., 1985)

[162]   *Something Beautiful for God*, by Malcolm Muggeridge (Collins, Fontana Books, 1972)

163 Thanks to Maggie Parham for quotes from her article "Help for the Handicapped" in *The Tablet,* April 29, 1994

164 *Maclean's Magazine*, article, September 4, 2000

165 *One Woman's Journey: A Portrait of Pauline Vanier* by Deborah Cowley and George Cowley (Novalis, 1993)

166 These quotes are from *Be Still and Listen* by Jean Vanier, (Daybreak Publications)

167 *Community of Love* by John Main (Darton, Longman and Todd, 1990)

168 *Ibid.*

169 From an article "Once a Mother, Always a Mother" by Fr. Patrick Eastman, *Monos Journal*, May 1993 (Tulsa, Oklahoma, USA)

170 *The Collected Works of St. John of the Cross* (Institute of Carmelite Studies, 1974)

171 *The Post-Charismatic Experience* by Robert Wild (Living Flame Press, 1984)

172 *New Seeds of Contemplation* by Thomas Merton (New Directions, 1949)

173 I am indebted to Father Charles Cummings, a Cistercian monk, for insights in this answer from his book *Spirituality and the Desert Experience* (Dimension Books, 1978)

174 *Silent Music* by William Johnston (Harper and Row, 1976)

175 *Thomas Merton on Prayer* edited by John J. Higgins SJ (Doubleday Image Books, 1975)

176 *Insight Meditation, the Practice of Freedom* by Joseph Goldstein (Shambhala Publications Inc.)

177 *Grace and Grit* by Ken Wilber (Shambhala Publications Inc., 1991)

178 *Prayer: Finding the Hearts True Home* by Richard J. Foster (Harper Collins, 1992) [author's italics]

179 *Letters From the Heart* by John Main (Crossroad, 1982)

180 *The Way of Unknowing* by John Main (Darton, Longman and Todd, 1989)

181 *The Complete Works of John of the Cross, Doctor of the Church* (Burns, Oates, 1943)

182 Excerpts for this question are from *Christian Meditation: Contemplative Prayer for a New Generation* by Paul Harris (Darton, Longman, Todd and Novalis, 1996)

183   *Our Family Magazine*, April 2000, an article "How to Forgive" by Victor M. Parachin

184   *The Present Christ* by John Main (Darton, Longman and Todd, 1984)

185   *Sharing the Journey* by Robert Wuthnow (The Free Press, 1994)

186   The *Christian Meditation Group: How to Start a Group, How to Lead a Group* by Laurence Freeman and Paul Harris (World Community for Christian Meditation, 1992)

187   *Sharing the Journey* by Robert Wuthnow (The Free Press, 1994)

188   *The Christian Meditation Group: How to Start a Group, How to Lead a Group* by Laurence Freeman and Paul Harris, (World Community for Christian Meditation, 1992)

189   "Mysticism, Nature and History" by Karl Rahner, *Encyclopedia of Theology* (Seabury Press, 1975)

190   *What is Contemplation?* by Thomas Merton (Templegate, 1981)

191   *The Hound of Heaven* by Francis Thompson (Morehouse-Barlow Co. Inc., 1980)

BIBLIOGRAPHY

Abhishiktananda, *Prayer*, ISPCK, 1967.

— *Ascent to the Depth of the Heart*, ISPCK, 1998.

Anonymous, *The Cloud of Unknowing* (Introduction by William Johnston), Doubleday, 1973.

Augustine Baker, *Holy Wisdom*, Burns and Oates, 1964.

New Catholic Encyclopedia Vol. 15, McGraw Hill, article on John Cassian, 1967.

John Cassian, *Conferences*, Paulist Press, 1985.

Catechism of the Catholic Church, Geoffrey Chapman, 1994.

Edmund Colledge and James Walsh, *Julian of Norwich: Showings*, Paulist Press, 1978.

A Course in Miracles, Foundation for Inner Peace, 1992.

Deborah Cowley and George Cowley, *One Woman's Journey: A Portrait of Pauline Vanier*. Novalis, 1993.

Charles Cummings, *Spirituality and the Desert Experience*, Dimension, 1978.

Odette Baumer-Despeigne, *The Spiritual Journey of Henry le Saux – Abhishiktananda*, Cistercian Studies, No. 4, 1983.

Louis Dupre and James A. Wiseman, *Light from Light: An Anthology of Christian Mysticism*, Paulist Press, 1988.

Patrick Eastman, *Once a Mother, Always a Mother*, Monos Journal, May 1993.

Eknath Easwaran, *Meditation, Commonsense Directions for an Uncommon Life*, Nilgiri Press, 1978.

— *The Unstruck Bell*, Nilgiri Press, 1993.

Meister Eckhart, *The Essential Sermon, Commentaries, Treatises and Defense*, Paulist Press and SPCK, 1981.

Laurence Freeman, *A Short Span of Days*, Novalis, 1991.

Laurence Freeman and Paul Harris, *The Christian Meditation Group: How to Lead a Group, How to Start a Group*, World Community for Christian Meditation, 1992.

R.M. French (trans.), *The Way of the Pilgrim*, Seabury Press, 1970.

Francois Gerard, *Going on a Journey*, privately printed, 1991.

Joseph Goldstein, *Insight Meditation, the Practice of Freedom*, Shambhala, 1993.

Carolyn Gratton, *The Art of Spiritual Guidance*, Crossroad, 1993.

Gregory of Nyssa, *The Life of Moses*, Paulist Press/SPCK, 1978.

Bede Griffiths, *Discovering the Feminine* (video), More Than Illusion Films, 1993.

— *The New Creation in Christ*, Darton, Longman and Todd, 1992.

— *The Golden String*, Collins Fount, 1979.

— *The Interface Between Christianity and Other Faiths*, (lecture), 1990.

— *The Marriage of East and West*, Collins Fount, 1983.

Paul Harris, *The Fire of Silence and Stillness: An Anthology of Quotations for the Spiritual Journey*, Darton, Longman and Todd and Templegate, 1995.

— *John Main by Those Who Knew Him*, Darton, Longman and Todd and Novalis, 1991.
Christian Meditation: Contemplative Prayer for a New Generation, Darton, Longman and Todd and Novalis, 1996.

— *The Heart of Silence*, Novalis and Darton, Longman and Todd, 1999.

— *Silence and Stillness in Every Season: Daily Readings with John Main*, Darton, Longman and Todd Continuum, 1997.

John J. Higgins, *Thomas Merton on Prayer*, Doubleday, 1973.

William James, *Varieties of Religious Experience*, The Modern Library, 1929.

John of the Cross, *The Collected Works of John of the Cross*, (Kavanaugh and Rodroguez (eds.), Institute of Carmelite Studies, 1974.

William Johnston, *Being in Love*, Collins, 1988.

— *The Inner Eye of Love*, Collins Fount, 1981.

— *The Mysticism of the Cloud of Unknowing*, Anthony Clarke Books and Abbey Press, 1975.

— *Silent Music*, Fontana, 1976.

Thomas Keating, *Intimacy With God*, Crossroad, 1994.

Soren Kierkegaard, *The Sickness Unto Death*, Princeton University Press, 1954.

William Law, *The Life of Christian Devotion*, Abingdon Press, 1961.

— *The Spirit of Love, Classics of Western Spirituality*, Paulist Press, 1978.

Kenneth Leech, *Soul Friend A Study of Spirituality*, Darton, Longman and Todd, 1974.

Andre Louf, *Teach Us to Pray*, Darton, Longman and Todd, new edition, 1991.

Neil McKenty, *In the Stillness Dancing*, Darton, Longman and Todd, 1986.

John Main, *Christian Meditation: The Gethsemani Talks*, World Community for Christian Meditation, 1977.

— *Community of Love*, Darton, Longman and Todd, 1990.

— *The Heart of Creation*, Darton, Longman and Todd, 1988.

— *The Inner Christ*, Darton, Longman and Todd, 1987.

— *Letters From the Heart*, Crossroad, 1982.

— *Moment of Christ*, Darton, Longman and Todd, 1984.

— *The Present Christ*, Darton, Longman and Todd, 1985.

— *Word into Silence*, Darton, Longman and Todd, 1980.

— *The Way of Unknowing*, Darton, Longman and Todd, 1989.

Vandana Mataji, *Swami Abhishiktananda: The Man and His Teaching*, SPCK, 1986.

Thomas Merton, *The Inner Experience*, Cistercian Studies, 1983-84.

— *Mystics and Zen Masters*, Dell, 1969.

— *New Seeds of Contemplation*, New Directions, 1962.

— *The Tears of the Blind Lions*, New Directions, 1949.

— *The Waters of Siloe*, Harcourt Brace, 1949.

— *The Way of Chuang Tzu*, New Directions, 1965.

— *What is Contemplation*, Templegate, 1950.

— *The Wisdom of the Desert*, New Directions, 1961.

E. Allison Peers, *The Complete Works of St. John of the Cross*, Burns, Oates and Washbourne, 1934.

Max Picard, *The World of Silence*, H. Regnery, 1988.

Antoine de Saint-Exupery, *The Little Prince*, Harcourt Brace and World, 1943.

William Shannon, *Thomas Merton's Dark Path*, Farrar, Straus and Giroux, 1987.

E.F. Schumacher, *Small is Beautiful*, Random House, 1989.

Madeleine Simon, *Born Contemplative*, Darton, Longman and Todd, 1993.

Cyprian Smith, *The Way of Paradox: Spiritual Life as Taught by Meister Eckhart*, Darton, Longman and Todd, 1987.

Mary Stewart and Giovanni Felicioni, *The Body in Meditation* (video), 1990.

Mother Teresa, *Mother Teresa, Contemplative in the Heart of the World*, Servant Books, 1985.

Jean Vanier, *Talks at the 1992 John Main Seminar*, World Community for Christian Meditation.

Vatican II, Decree of the Church's Missionary Activity, *Ad Gentes*, 1965.

— Declaration on the Relation of the Church to Non-Christian Religions, *Nostra Aetate*, 1967.

Kallistos Ware, *Theology and Prayer*, Fellowship of St. Alban and St. Sergius.

Ken Wilber, *Grace and Grit*, Shambhala, 1991.

Robert Wild, *Enthusiasm in the Spirit*, Ave Maria Press, 1975.

— *The Post-Charismatic Experience*, Living Flame Press, 1984.

NAME INDEX

Other books on Christian Meditation

The Heart of Silence

Contemplative Prayer by Those Who Practise It
Paul Harris

In a world increasingly aware of the need for inner stillness, the 60 meditators in this book speak about a path of
prayer that is anchored in both Christian tradition and
contemplative experience, that is ever new: a path beyond
words, thoughts and imagination into the presence of the
risen Lord who dwells in our hearts in silence.

• paperback
• 224 pages

Christian Meditation

Contemplative Prayer for a New Generation
Paul Harris

Drawing on the teaching of Scripture and of Dom John
Main, this book provides novices and experienced meditators alike with instruction and encouragement for the
contemplative journey.

• paperback
• 146 pages

Silence and Stillness in Every Season

Daily Readings with John Main

Paul Harris

This book presents John Main's teaching, drawn from all his published works, in an attractive daily readings format.

- paperback
- 384 pages

Christian Meditation

Your Daily Practice

Laurence Freeman, OSB

- paperback
- 80 pages

A concise handbook by a highly-respected expert on meditation – practical and inspirational.

ALL AVAILABLE FROM NOVALIS 1-800-387-7164
cservice@novalis.ca